1001 Success Secrets

Secrets Exposed from eBay Millionaires

GLOBAL PUBLISHING GROUP

Global Publishing Group

Australia • New Zealand • Singapore • America • London

1001 eBay Success Secrets

Secrets Exposed from eBay Millionaires

"Brilliant Book, Full of Step by Step easy to follow Money-Making Strategies that will make you Rich."
Darren Stephens, Best Selling Author of *"The Success Principles"*

Matt & Amanda Clarkson
World's Leading eBay Educators

DISCLAIMER

All the information, techniques, skills and concepts contained within this publication are of the nature of general comment only and are not in any way recommended as individual advice. The intent is to offer a variety of information to provide a wider range of choices now and in the future, recognising that we all have widely diverse circumstances and viewpoints. Should any reader choose to make use of the information contained herein, this is their decision, and the contributors (and their companies), authors and publishers do not assume any responsibilities whatsoever under any condition or circumstances. It is recommended that the reader obtain their own independent advice.

SECOND EDITION 2011

National Library of Australia
Cataloguing-in-Publication entry:

Clarkson, Matt, 1971-
1001 eBay Success Secrets – Secrets Exposed from eBay Millionaires

2nd ed.
ISBN: 978-1-921630-61-3 (pbk.)

ebay
Internet Auctions
Internet Marketing
Electronic commerce
Success in business

Cataloguing Number pending

Published by Global Publishing Group
PO Box 517 Mt Evelyn, Victoria 3796 Australia
Email info@TheGlobalPublishingGroup.com

For Further information about orders:
Phone: +61 3 9736 1156 or Fax +61 3 8648 6871

GLOBAL PUBLISHING GROUP

Foreword

THE International Achievement INSTITUTE

Bringing Essential Knowledge & Book Summaries to High Achievers

I would like to personally congratulate you on investing in this valuable book. At The International Achievement Institute we continually strive to create excellence in the business world. And so it is with great pleasure that I write the foreword for this book. I believe it is a fantastic resource for anyone interested in making money or involved in business either as a start up or established business.

The online industry is one that is leading this country into greater economic prosperity and is central to the health of our economy. It is also an industry that is bringing incredible wealth and personal fulfilment to those involved in it. Critical to the success of our industry, its credibility, and its ability to weather the economic storms that may come, is not just good systems and methods, but most importantly good solid relationships.

Good relationships are, I believe, the difference between an outstanding business system and one that fails. I have seen this time and time again. And that is why this book is so valuable; because it is about people and their personal stories. Without the people behind them and their personal approach to relationships, a business owner is doomed to failure. With successful business-savvy people who know that 'relationship is king' involved in an eBay business, then the sky is the limit.

By learning from others and their mistakes you can be light years ahead of your competition. You can save hundreds of thousands of dollars simply by avoiding the mistakes they made and learned from.

The International Achievement Institute is proud to recommend this book as its authors are world leading eBay experts with many years of experience. They have taken on the ultimate challenge, made mistakes along the way, kept growing professionally and personally, and now enjoy incredible success.

As an International best selling author & consultant myself, I've had the privilege to consult and work with tens of thousands of people from Presidents, Rock stars, fortune 500 executives to every day people from all walks of life from over 27 countries.

For a few years I'd watched eBay growing as a company and I still didn't think of eBay as a serious business opportunity; I merely thought of it as a online junk yard. That was until I met Matt & Amanda Clarkson.

No business venture is without some level of risk, but by becoming more educated and informed you can reduce those risks so that they are far outweighed by the possible benefits.

This book will offer you just that information. It is an inspiring read and one that will make you want to jump out of your seat, leap out of your comfort zone and take action. And I encourage you to do just that.

Darren J. Stephens
Chief Executive Officer
The International Achievement Institute

The road to success starts with one simple step forward and the burning desire to see your dreams become reality…even in times of adversity and doubt.

In this book, you'll discover our 1001 eBay Success Secrets that have taken us from broke to eBay Millionaires within two years and allowed us the freedom to inspire and help others who want the eBay lifestyle too. We continue to live by these success secrets daily.

To get the most out of this book, keep it close and handy for those moments when you need guidance, answers, tips & inspiration from those who have blazed the trail before you…Enjoy.

To your eBay Success!

Matt & Amanda Clarkson

Acknowledgements

Following the huge success of our first best seller *The Magic Of Making Money On eBay*, we knew there was so much more we wanted to share with you. Creating the *1001 eBay Success Secrets* was our way of sharing the tips, strategies and mantras we use that will help you reach your goals faster and more easily.

As with any major project or business success, there are many very special people who have contributed to our growth, making it possible for us to achieve our goals, and ultimately to making this book happen. So we'd like to take this opportunity to say "THANK YOU".

Firstly, we'd like to thank you and our thousands of eBay Magic members who were the inspiration for writing this book.

Next, a huge thanks to our wonderful team here at Bidding Buzz who supported us while we worked tirelessly to coordinate and pull all the material together for this book, as well as our ongoing efforts to spread the word on what's possible with an eBay business.

You're like family to us... you all know who you are. You're an outstanding team and are the glue that holds this wild ride together!

A heartfelt thank you to our awesome publisher, Global Publishing Group, for your dedication and commitment to the book's success. You go far beyond what's expected and without you this book would not have happened!

We thank our friends and partners Darren & Jackie Stephens for your amazing talent, feedback, support and laughter when we need it most. Mostly, we thank you for being you...honourable.

Contents

Contents

Introduction

Why You Simply Can't Afford NOT To Be Selling On eBay… …And How Learning Our Secret Tips And Strategies Will Give You The Edge You Need To Be In The Top 5% Of eBay Sellers Who Make The Real Money & Live The Life Most People Only Dream About…

If you're just starting out on eBay, or if you already have an eBay business, the good news is that this is just the beginning. eBay has only been up and running since 1995, and what started out as a website for people to sell antiques on has become a worldwide phenomenon.

What this means for everyday people like you and us is that we are getting involved right at the beginning in a sense, and only time will tell how big this opportunity will grow. What I do know though, is that there has never been an easier or faster way to make extra streams of income than using eBay as a wealth vehicle.

Because eBay is still very young as a business, not all individuals or businesses are selling online yet. We doubt there's a single person out there who hasn't heard of eBay, or how everyday people are becoming "stay at home internet millionaires" through their eBay business.

What started out as an experiment in 1995 by a man named Pierre Omidyar became the world's largest personal online trading community.

Introduction

Did you know around 52,000 Australians are making their income from selling on eBay? Will you be next?

A few years ago, many considered eBay as a big "garage sale" instead of a legitimate business. These days, selling on eBay has become somewhat of a craft where many savvy sellers are making a fortune! What it comes down to is treating your eBay business as a "real business" and not a part-time hobby. You will learn more about this as you read on.

You've only got to read the newspapers and magazines to see stories of "everyday" folks like you and us who become "eBay Success Stories." Everyday consumers are also making the transition to buying things on eBay and the Internet and are getting way more comfortable with the whole idea and concept of online shopping. In fact, some are even addicted to it!

Did you know that more than 70,000 new members join eBay every day? Most of them are buyers. As of writing this book, there are around 276 million registered members on eBay. About 86 million of them are active buyers spending in excess of 1 Billion dollars a week. Around 1.3 million of these people are sellers. Can you see an opportunity for you to start selling on eBay too?

According to Forrester Research in 2009, a massive $23 Billion was spent online in 2008. They predict that by 2012, online spending will reach $72 Billion. That's not even including what is currently selling on eBay, which really shows you just how massive this opportunity already is.

5.35 Million people visited eBay Australia in June 2009. As of writing this book, there are around 8 million unique registered eBay users in

Australia. People's spending habits are slowly changing too, from the majority being Auction, now the breakdown is around 50% Auction format and 50% Buy It Now format.

Did you know that there are literally dozens of ways to market your business on eBay and many different selling options, depending on what you want out of having an eBay business? In fact, we'll share 12 of them with you in this book.

Most people don't have a clue about most of the selling options and the great thing about that is, if you take advantage of what we'll share with you, chances are you'll be on the road to profits faster and more easily than you ever imagined.

You're about to discover some strategies and methods that will set you apart from any competitor in your chosen field. By miles! Whether you're intending on cleaning out your garage or spare room, OR looking to start a serious and lucrative moneymaking venture, eBay makes it super simple for you.

All you need is an open mind, self-belief and a desire like nothing else to take control of your own financial and personal destiny for you and your family.

There is just one more thing however... Making money on eBay can become *extremely* addictive, so be warned. ☺

Matt & Amanda

"The Internet is changing everything, and has changed the world in such a short period of time, and will continue to change things in very positive ways that we have yet to anticipate."

Pierre Omidyar
Billionaire & founder of eBay

Chapter 1

With So Much To Learn Where Do You Start?

Chapter 1: With So Much To Learn...

1. It's all about having the edge right from the start. Here's where most sellers get it wrong and wonder why they can't make a decent profit on eBay. Coming from a business background, in my opinion, it's not worth going into business of any sort unless you know what you're doing from the start or are prepared to learn quickly.

2. Start with the end in mind and then work your way backwards to achieve your goals whilst you're learning the ropes.

3. It can seem daunting starting any new career or business and you must always keep in mind that Rome wasn't built in a day! Write down a list of tasks you need to accomplish so you're going in with a clear plan of action.

4, Less can be more on eBay. You may only learn one new task every day, but it's best to master each step before moving on to the next step. Set yourself achievable goals and tasks that you will be able to complete. The goal posts can always be moved when you reach them!

5. Sometimes your goals can make you feel overwhelmed. If this is the case, break them down into 'bite sizes' to manage one task at a time. There are many daily activities you'll be doing in your eBay business that eventually you can automate. When we first started out, we wrote down all the daily tasks and split them between us.

6. We worked out who was best at what, divided them up and then took responsibility for the tasks each day. By 11am we were finished for the day and, best of all, we worked harmoniously *(most of the time ;-)* because we knew exactly what needed to be done!

7. If you're planning on working with your 'life partner' and building your eBay business together, it's a great idea to plan your "outcome" together so you can avoid killing each other along the way! Seriously… if you're on the same path, your journey is going to be a whole lot more enjoyable, so take the time to talk it through as you may be "thinking" completely different strategies without knowing it!

8. If you're in business with someone, stick to the tasks you're best at and try to hand off those you're not so great at. We did this from the start (even though we were a jack-of-all-trades at the beginning), which made growing our eBay business much more fun.

9. Never go into any business without thinking about what it is you'd like to get out of it long term. Is it more money? More time with your family, peace of mind, having your own business? Etc., etc…

10. Being unclear about exactly what it is that you want will make your goals and dreams seem unrealistic and out of reach.

11. If you don't know how to set goals, take some time out and think about what your perfect day, week, month and year would look like. Then create your business around those images you have in your mind's eye.

12. Don't share your goals and dreams with anyone who you know will laugh or ridicule you. It's not worth it. If you have no one to share them with, keep a journal and write in it every day.

13. Creating the perfect business and lifestyle can seem like a feat only for the strong… however if you have a big enough 'dream' you too will find a way. We are constantly blown away by how people we mentor start out 'down and out' and go on to create amazing eBay businesses and amazing lifestyles to match.

14. There are many reasons why people go into business… too many to name here; however, I can tell you that nearly every one of them just wants more choices in life… what do you want?

Married Mum With New Born Baby Makes $2614 In First Month…And Counting

Hi Matt & Amanda,

I want to say a huge thank you! I'm loving your eBay Magic course. I thoroughly enjoy going through the manuals and CD's, and you make it **so simple and straightforward to follow**. I've had the material for about 4 weeks now and I've started by selling things from around the house, as you suggested.
I'm up to **$2,613.00** and I honestly think I'll be able to reach over $4,000 in the next few weeks. It's addictive! I love logging on and seeing whose bid, how many people are watching. I'm having great fun and making money.

A fabulous investment.

Monique. M

"Its in moments of decision your destiny is create."

Darren J Stephens
International Bestselling Author & Speaker

Chapter 2

Getting Started On eBay And Deciding What To Sell

Chapter 2: Getting Started...

15. Starting A Profitable and Automated eBay Business From Scratch Has Never Been So Simple Or Achievable. By Following A Proven, Simple Step-By-Step Formula, You Can Be Making Your First Profits Within Days Of Starting!

16. Depending on what style of eBay business you set up and what you want to achieve from having it will determine how and where you end up sourcing your products long term.

17. If you're happy to be an eBay hobbyist and make extra income on the side, you'll probably end up sourcing most of your stock locally from places like flea markets, garage sales, second-hand shops and places like this.

18. If you want to set up a more sustainable, automated eBay business, you will need to think about sourcing suppliers that can supply you on an ongoing basis.

19. When starting out, don't panic about what products you'll sell long term. When we first starting selling on eBay, we were clueless! In fact, during the first 3 months we basically sold everything that wasn't nailed down while we were researching what we wanted to sell long term. The best part… we were earning while we were learning!

20. In the early stages, once you run out of things to sell around the house, ask your friends and family. Go to opportunity shops, flea markets and second-hand dealers, and bookstores too! We even bought second-hand shoes and sold them on eBay. We did this all the time in the early

days and they'd all laugh at us!
Yeah, well they're not laughing anymore that's for sure! J

21. In the early days, while you're'earning as you're learning the ropes', it's a great idea to think about exactly what you'd like to achieve from having your eBay business. Will this be a hobby where you make extra income on the side, or would you eventually like to make a full-time income?

22. Thinking your business needs through will give you more ideas of what types of things you may want to sell on an ongoing basis. You'll learn more about what we mean as you read on and see all the pieces of the jigsaw puzzle coming together.

23. When you start selling on eBay, it's important to begin by selling small low-cost items first. You want to learn the ropes on items that are not expensive and you won't be too disappointed if they sell really cheap. It's important to build yourself a'track record' for selling on eBay so buyers will trust you.

24. If you start by selling items that are too expensive, you actually run the risk of having your account suspended by eBay. This is because eBay is very much focused on protecting the seller from fraudsters and bad shopping experiences.

25. If you haven't sold on eBay before, build up your feedback by selling old DVDs and CDs, books and old clothes before you even consider selling medium or high-ticket items long term. Focus on building up your feedback score while

gaining experience, and not so much on the dollar value, at this early stage of your future empire.

Chapter 3
eBay Basics - Opening Your Accounts

Chapter 3: eBay Basics...

26. To get started on eBay, you'll need to register an account, which is very simple. All eBay require is some personal info, a credit card and an email address. You must also be over 18 years of age and agree to their user agreement terms and privacy policy.

27. There are two types of accounts you can register on eBay, which are A) a personal account or B) a business account. If you're not already trading as a company, a personal account is fine for most people.

28. On the other hand, if you already have a company and want to use the company details for your eBay account, your company information will be displayed to buyers instead of your individual information.

29. Regardless of which type of account you set up, you'll need to choose a User Id (eBay name) that sounds professional.

30. When choosing your eBay user ID, it's a good idea not to pick numerals, symbols or letters that your customers may not remember. For instance, John_12098 is not a good idea because if someone were trying to promote you as a great eBay seller, never in a million years would they remember your user ID!

31. Pick something easy for the everyday person to remember, as most eBay businesses are built on word of mouth. Getting this right upfront will make you far more profits in the long term.

32. You can change your eBay User Id every 30 days and retain your feedback score; however, it's best to choose a name that sounds professional from the start so there's no need to change it.

33. eBay has created a great page called 'My eBay' to keep track of all your buying and selling data in one location, which means you can keep track of your sales with ease.

34. Did you know 'My eBay' is personalised to your specific browsing, buying and selling activities and you can tailor the layout? You can customize the summary view by choosing to include or exclude various sections to only view a one-page snapshot of all your activities.

35. To see how much money you have made since you last visited eBay, just log in to My eBay 'Sold' view to see your most recent sales. My eBay is your complete snapshot view of your business at any given moment.

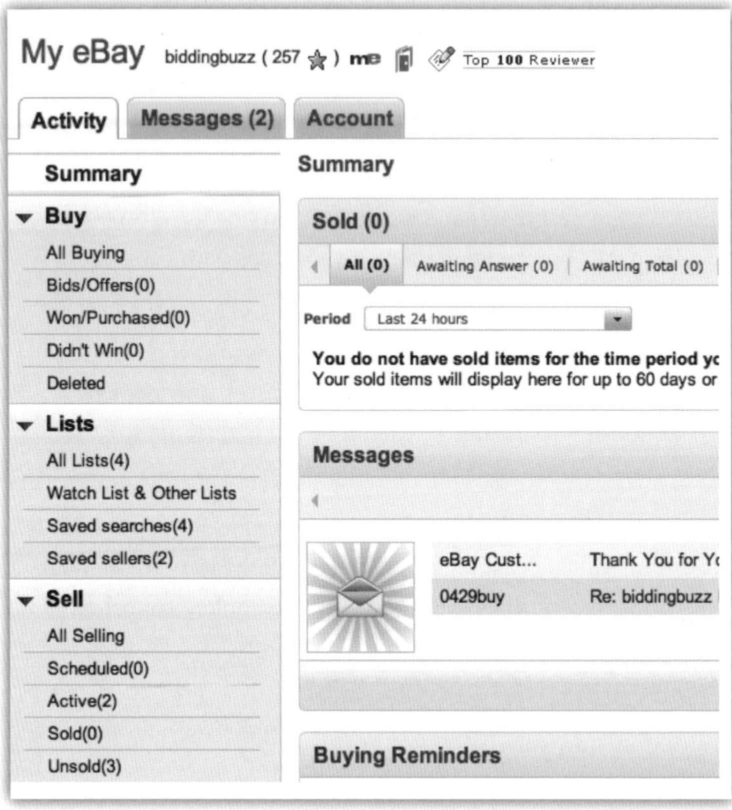

36. When you're first starting out, it may seem like there are so many different sections in 'My eBay', so click on them one by one and you'll soon discover where it takes you!

37. To make sure your customer service is up to date, frequently check your 'My Messages' in eBay. The quicker you answer questions from buyers, the more likely they are to buy from you and come back to shop with you.

38. My eBay features a 'Shortcuts' menu on the left-hand side of the page that you can customise. To add links to the eBay pages you use the most or to delete those you don't, click the 'Edit Shortcuts' button.

39 You can save time and work more efficiently by saving searches, stores and sellers in 'My eBay'.

40. If you want to update or remove any of your personal and financial information, you just need to go to the 'Account' tab in My eBay.

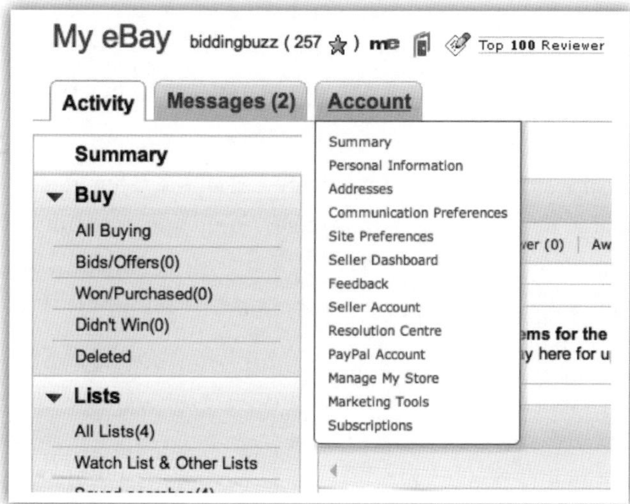

41. 'My eBay' includes many icons for helping you quickly view the status of listings, transactions, messages, and feedback. These icons will change colour when different actions are performed.

42. You can view the 'Legend' at the bottom of the page to see what the icons mean.

43. Did you know there are thousands and thousands of categories and sub-categories you can sell into on eBay? In fact, there are around 50 thousand main categories you can start on even before you hit the sub-categories within! Don't ever let anyone talk you into believing eBay is flooded with sellers! It's just not true and there's plenty of room for you my friend.

44. A great way to familiarise yourself with all the categories available to list your item in is to click on the 'Buy' button to explore all the levels and see which is most suitable. This is just one way you can explore the many opportunities for selling on eBay.

45. Many buyers search for items to purchase through the categories, so it's vital that you list your items in the correct categories, regardless of what categories other sellers are using!

46. Remember that most sellers on eBay don't know half the tips that we're sharing with you in this book, so if you copy other sellers, you're more than likely copying their mistakes too.

47. Avoid listing in two categories, as you will be charged extra insertion fees. As long as you are listing your item in the most suitable category with great titles, you won't need to pay for multiple categories.

48. To choose an appropriate category for your item, make sure you use the most specific keywords to describe it, as you'll attract more buyers.

49. eBay may move your listing if it appears in a category that is unrelated to the item you are selling.

50. In our experience, listing your item in one category (if you pick the correct one) will get you more targeted buyers than listing over two categories, and in the end give you more profits.

51. When you first start selling on eBay, Auctions will be the most common selling format you should use because you want to 'pump' out the listings to get your feedback built as quickly as possible.

52. In the early days of starting your eBay business, because you haven't yet built credibility with your buyers, (in the way of your feedback score) they often won't trust you or spend large amounts of money with you.

53 When you first start out and you're wondering what to sell, it's a good idea to sell everything you don't want that's lying around the house. Start with smaller things that you no longer want or need, rather than items that you want good money for.

54. You're going to make mistakes along the way. This is normal and it's how you deal with the mistakes that will either make or break your business.

55. Mistakes are another reason why it's vital to sell items you're not attached to when building up your feedback so you can learn from them before sourcing ongoing products.

56. We started slowly and began all of our auctions at 99 cents. We sold books, DVDs, Videos, CDs, Cassettes and the like. We weren't attached to any of it, which made it all the more fun. We were making great profits from day one!

57. Because eBay is well known for its auction style, as a seller it's best practice to let the market dictate what something is worth, rather than putting a starting price on the auction that you think the product is worth.

58. By starting the auction at the lowest possible price you're willing to take for it, (after you have built your feedback) allows buyers to 'bid' the price up. In lot's of cases you can make even more than you hoped for because you might start a bidding frenzy!

59. When bids are placed, eBay uses a program called 'Proxy Bidding' to bid on the buyer's behalf. They increase the auction price in increments of 50¢, which is automatically determined based on the next highest current bid.

60. As you become more familiar with Auctions, you can also add 'Buy It Now' prices alongside of the Auction price, but be warned if someone bids on the Auction price, the Buy It Now price will vanish.

61. Be careful if any buyers ask you to end your item early before the Auction has time to run its course. They may think that you don't know the true value of your item and may be trying to get a bargain.

62 Savvy buyers wait until the last minute of the Auction to 'snipe' a bargain, so you won't know how much you might be able to get for your item until the Auction has ended.

63. Not only is it annoying for any prospects that may be watching your item to bid on, but ending items and selling them off eBay early is not allowed and you can get your account suspended or permanently cancelled, so don't even go there!

64. Auctions are ideal to start your items at a low price and watch the buyers out there bid the price up until the allocated time/days expires. This is a great way to see what buyers in the eBay world are prepared to pay for things they want.

65. Whilst Auctions are the most common listing format, buyers are now also moving towards the 'Buy it Now' format because they want instant gratification. It's your mission as a seller to give them what they want. Do this, and you'll get what you want—a thriving eBay business!

66. You do need to be realistic with your pricing when listing Buy It Now items, because if they're set too high no one will buy them; however if they're set too low, then you'll not only be losing money, you'll also be setting the standard for that item.

67. Because Buy It Now items can take the fun out of bidding, you can still negotiate the Buy It Now price by accepting 'Best Offers'.

68. Best Offers are great as they offer buyers the opportunity to haggle with you a little. The buyer can still feel like they're getting a bargain, as they may be saving a few dollars off of the set amount.

69. From experience, most buyers will only offer a small discounted amount, usually around 10% or less, and the beauty with Best Offers is that you can automate them, so you don't even have to be online to negotiate the prices with your potential buyer!

70. You can set the lowest and highest price you're willing to accept as an offer and the system will automatically send a reply to your buyer.

71. By using the Best Offer tool, you can also see what the buyers out there in the eBay world are prepared to pay for your item, rather than demanding what you want for the item.

72. eBay also rewards sellers that sell the same product on an ongoing basis by showing your listings higher up in the search results, which are sorted by what eBay consider a 'Best Match', rather than items simply ending soonest.

73. Best Match uses specific algorithms to help your listing be seen at the top of the page. Your sales history counts in this instance, so adding a 'quantity' (of items) in your listing can be more beneficial to your overall visibility.

74. Did you know that if you list items using the multiple-quantity format, and you've made sales from the same listing in recent days, you'd build up a sales history that will help boost your listing's position in the search results?

75. If you have a quantity of a product, instead of using individual listings, you can use one fixed price listing to list a number of them so you can retain your sales history and boost your Best Match position.

76. Regardless of which selling method you decide is best for your listing, it's imperative that your buyer doesn't realise you have a never-ending supply of stock, because this will not give them any 'urgency' to bid!

77. Specify in your quantity that you have a small number of products to promote scarcity, or set your account settings up to show 'More than 10 available' rather than the true number of items you have in stock.

78. Ideally, if you have a never-ending supply of items, you'd have one of each selling method in use to test and measure the market.

79. You can also make more sales by sending out 'Second Chance Offers' to those who miss out on winning your Auctions, because you can email the next highest bidders and give them the opportunity to purchase your item at their maximum bidding price.

80. Let's say you had 10 identical items in stock and 10 different buyers bid on your item, you can offer the 9 buyers that missed out a 'Second Change Offer.' The best part is you only pay the one insertion fee for selling all 10 items in one go! How good's that!

81. Second Chance Offers can be sent out manually after a sale is made or even be set up to be sent automatically. However, make sure only to use the second chance offer if the bidders have all bid over a price you are happy with.

82. Try and send out second chance offers as soon as possible, because buyers will be disappointed they lost the auction and will move on to another item quickly.

83. Be conscious of what duration you select for the 'Second Chance Offer' to be available to your buyers, because if

it's too short, the buyer may not get time to see the offer. However if the duration is too long, there'll be no urgency for the buyer to purchase it.

84. Second Chance Offers are also one of the easiest ways to move inventory faster and increase your eBay auction cash flow and profits, allowing multiple sales from just one listing!

85. You need to think about how long your items should be listed for and what day and time they're going to end to target your specific market.

86. Did you know that choosing the correct duration for your listing can mean the difference between getting the greatest amount of bids or not being seen?

87. When you're first starting out and aren't sure of the best durations, 7- 10 days generally works best, so you can get the most amount of eyeballs (Traffic) on your listing!

88. With auctions and fixed priced listings, you can list your items with durations of 1, 3, 5, 7 or 10 days.

89. One-day durations are mostly used when selling tickets, vouchers and items that need to be claimed by a certain date. To use a one-day listing duration, you also need to have a feedback score of 5, have a PayPal account in good standing and also accept PayPal as a payment method.

90. If your item is related to a certain event (for example, a ticket for a concert or a holiday gift), you should choose a listing ending time that would give you enough time to ship the item to the buyer before the holiday or event takes place.

91. Sometimes it's best to choose a one day or three day auction for your item. This encourages bidders to act quickly if they're there for the thrill of a fast auction and outbidding the competition at the last moment!

92. When two or more hours have passed since you submitted the listing, you won't be able to change the duration of your listing.

93. Make sure you know the popularity of the item you are listing, so you can use the best listing durations possible.

94. Because bidding and buying on eBay is an enjoyable experience, you'll occasionally notice buyers get caught up in the hype and excitement and then don't actually go through with the sale. This is generally a very small percentage of sales and a perfect time to consider sending out a second chance offer rather than re-listing the item and paying the insertion fee again.

95. If you do encounter a 'non paying' bidder, it's important to inform eBay. This is to ensure that they're not doing this on a regular basis; otherwise eBay has the right to suspend or cancel their account.

96. You can block buyers from bidding on or purchasing your items by specifying buyer requirements through the 'sell your item form in eBay'.

97. Blocking buyers can be helpful if they have several unpaid items recorded on their account of violations, this may stop them from doing the same to you.

98. Customers with 0 or under 10 feedback can be blocked on your listings if they are high-ticket items and you're not sure if you can trust them as yet.

99. While selecting buyer requirements may reduce your exposure to buyers who could make transactions difficult, it can also reduce the number of potential buyers for your items, so use them wisely.

100. The buyer requirements you select will be applied to all your current and future listings, but can be disabled anytime if a buyer contacts you and requests to bid on your items in advance.

101. Phone verification is great to set up in buyer requirements if you're selling in a high scam category, such as electronics, laptops and mobile phones.

102. Keep in mind that some buyers may have a legitimate reason for not going through with a sale and everyone deserves a second chance, so don't be too harsh!

103. eBay is built on the 'feedback system.' This means that you're basically judged for your service and offerings by the people who buy from you. Your eBay seller ratings are

public and most buyers look at this information before they buy from you to gauge what you are like as a seller.

104. Feedback is the score you see next to your eBay User ID... this score is kept for as long as you have an active eBay account and one feedback score is given each time you sell or buy on eBay.

105. Your feedback score is vital to your eBay business. As there is often no verbal or physical communication, your feedback score is the only way for a buyer to gauge your reputation and the history of your past transactions with other buyers, so that they feel confident and comfortable in purchasing from you.

106. In the early stages, it may seem like a slow boat to China to build your feedback; however, it's one of the most important stages of growing a long-term successful eBay Business.

107. In the early days, you are simply growing your reputation as a great eBay seller by building your feedback so that other buyers will want to buy from you.

108. There are several components with the feedback you receive as a seller, and if you desire to run a successful eBay business, it's imperative for you to maintain your Feedback at the highest level possible. This will not only allow you to be viewed as a reputable seller, it also shows eBay that you are abiding by their rules...and, most importantly, it shows other buyers what the experience has been like for your previous customers.

109. Not everyone who buys from you will leave feedback, and as it forms a large portion of your eBay Business and credibility, it's always best to ask for it to be given. Sometimes you need to prompt buyers a couple of times to leave you Feedback.

110. You can also set up the process of leaving feedback automatic to your customers, again saving you time from having to do tasks that can be automated.

111. As a seller, you can no longer give your buyers negative or neutral feedback as of 2008 when the rules changed. Most sellers were up in arms; however, it has forced sellers to raise their game and do the right thing by buyers. If you do everything in your power to uphold the eBay rules and give outstanding service, you can build a great business on eBay and enjoy the rewards and benefits this brings.

112. Our advice for new eBay sellers is to build your feedback score up to 100 positive feedbacks as fast as you can by being a seller, not a buyer. You see, buyers want to know what other people's experience has been like shopping with you before they make a decision to buy from you.

113. Go for it…you can get to 100 very quickly once you get cracking and 100 is seen as the magic feedback number. Once you hit the triple digits, you should find your items get better end prices as your customers will perceive you as a credible, established and trustworthy seller.

114. Never make the mistake and think that you can 'buy' your way to 100 feedbacks. Not only can this be costly, but

your future prospects can see that you have bought your feedback, which looks unprofessional.

115. Purchasing stationery such as bubble wrap and the odd thing here and there is ok and can save you a few dollars on packaging, but don't get addicted; you're here to make money, not spend it!

116. As a buyer, never leave negative feedback for the seller until you have given them the opportunity of fixing the problem first. If you purchase a physical item from a shop, would you return to the shop first to see if they can fix the problem?

117. Your feedback is so important on eBay and is the foundation to having a long-term lucrative business, so ask your buyers for it and always be polite when asking for feedback and never demand it, or you may get neutral or negative feedback as a result!

118. You can print up a simple thank you card and ask politely for feedback. Include this card with the items you sell to try and encourage your seller to leave you feedback.

119. You can also email your buyers reminders to leave you feedback because not every buyer will automatically realise you're waiting for them to do so.

120. If you sell multiple products to the same buyer in a 7 day period, this will only be classed as one 'feedback point' which is why you need to list lots of items regularly and sell a variety of products in the early days.

121. When we started selling on eBay back in February 2006, we would have a minimum of 50 items up for sale at any given time. By doing this, we were practically guaranteed of a regular weekly income and were well on our way to 100 feedbacks. Back then, we were making hundreds of dollars a week profit, just from selling our 'unwanted stuff' from around the house.

122. As your feedback score grows, you'll see a different colour star next to your User ID and there are 12 different colours available, right through to a silver shooting star when you reach a humble 1 million feedback points!

123. The most important part of any listing you create should be the 'Keywords' in your title because this is how potential buyers will be able to find your widgets for sale.

124. Your title is made up of 55 characters, which includes spaces, punctuation and any letters, so make the most of them! It's a fact that 54% of listings on eBay don't get a single bid and this isn't because no one's searching for that item... it's because sellers don't understand the power of using 'rich' keywords.

125. Just to give you an idea of how many sellers don't fathom the concept of using 'rich keywords' in their titles, a search on the word 'wow' had 4,573 listings, the word 'gorgeous' 17,144 listings and the word "beautiful" 17,350 listings! Now I don't know about you, but I have never searched for these keywords when shopping!

126. Just because you call your widget one name, that doesn't mean that others out there (especially in different countries) will call it the same thing! For example, purse, wallet and clutch could all refer to the same thing.

127. Use keywords that buyers are actively searching for, rather than the obvious names you're familiar with, and there are great programs that are on the market that will help you with keywords such as: **http://tinyurl.com/BiddingBuzzTerapeak**

terapeak™ marketplace research Research eBay, Sell Smarter!

128. Subtitles on the other hand, are not keyword rich, which means that they won't help your buyers find your products in the search engines.

129. At a current cost of AU 49¢ per listing, subtitles can eat into your profits if not used wisely.

130. Remember, when selling online, buyers can't touch and feel the item as they would in a normal retail-buying environment, so your listing descriptions must give plenty of information to be able to make the decision to buy from you!

131. Taking great photos of what you're selling will maximize your profits every single time and leave your competitors in the dust!

132. As a seller, you need to make your listings look super attractive to encourage buyers to take action and place a bid.

133. Photos play a huge role on eBay, and if you have poor, blurry, unprofessional looking photos, buyers won't want to shop with you.

134. Adding images to a listing creates more views and significantly improves your chances of a successful sale. And with good reason... would you buy a product you couldn't look at first?

135. You've heard the saying… 'A picture paints a thousand words' and it's never been a truer saying when it comes to selling on eBay. The photos you put in your eBay listing can and will make or break your business when it comes to the bottom line.

136. Even if what you're selling has some minor (or major) defects, be sure to show them in the photos. You'd be surprised at how many buyers don't mind dents, dings and scratches on items as long as you've been upfront about it from the start.

137. Remember to take photos of the good, the bad and the ugly angles of your item, without photographing it in a way that will surprise your buyer when it arrives and looks completely different from the listing!

138. When possible, instead of taking your photos with a flash, use natural daylight, as this will bring out the colours and details much better.

139. Try to limit the background distractions so customers can easily see what it is that you are selling. There's nothing worse than having to guess what it is you're buying!

140. You'd be surprised at some of the pictures we've seen sellers use in their listings. A lot of the time, you can't even tell what the seller is selling for the junk in the background!

141. Never drape the item over the driveway, armchair or any other prop! Use a plain white wall or sheet for your background, or if you're more advanced you can even remove the background with photo editing software.

142. If you're selling things like clothing, often you'll fetch more for your items if you have a real person modelling them or you can even invest in a mannequin. It'll be money well spent.

143. Until you perfect the photographing process, you can edit it or improve it with basic photo-editing software, such as Paint or Windows Photo Gallery.

144. Simple changes such as cropping out the excess background or lightening the picture can massively improve your listings, but never alter the condition or colour of your item or your buyers could feel misled and leave you negative feedback.

145. A great idea is to set up an area to take your photos in and leave it set up for greater ease. Maybe a spare room in your home, the garage or basement, if there's enough light. This way, your photographing time will be reduced because you won't waste any time clearing space to take photos in each time.

146. Depending on your camera settings, some formats are too large to upload directly to eBay, so check your camera manual to avoid buyers having trouble viewing your photos.

147. It's currently free to insert the first photo on eBay and then AU 25¢ per photo afterwards, so the amount of pictures you use in your listing will depend on the value of the item you're selling.

148. In order for buyers to view your photos on the Internet, eBay needs to 'host' the photos online, which is why they charge you per photo.

149. Using outside picture hosting programs can and will see you stand out from the crowd when selling on eBay. Don't forget... you want every edge you can get in this business.

150. One of the best programs to host your photos with minimal outlay is **www.auctiva.com**, or if you're more advanced you can host them on your own server.

151. eBay also has their own hosting program called 'eBay's Picture Services' that you can use to host your photos when you create a listing.

152. Be wise when deciding what company you're going to use to host your photos. An unreliable host can make your listings suffer and may bring down your profits if the photos take too long to load or don't look professional.

153. Did you know that you can also protect your images so no one else uses them just by watermarking them in editing programs? This is great when you have ongoing products to sell, especially if your competition gets any ideas.

Married Homemaker Mother Of Three Makes $1500 In First Weeks

This is the best money I have spent on myself to date. Within 1 month of starting the eBay Magic course I'd made $1500 and that was just the kids room! Now I don't even have to think about school fees this term. Wait till I get to that garage!

5 weeks into it, I've now found the product that I'm going to source and sell long term, thanks to Matt & Amanda's help.

By August I'll be making enough money so that my husband Matt can cut hours & the real living will begin for us as a family. Because that IS what it's all about isn't it?

Thanks for always walking by my side Matt & Amanda, I can't say thank you enough!

Danielle T, Sydney

Success is neither magical nor mysterious. Success is the natural consequence of consistently applying basic fundamentals.

Jim Rohn
Bestselling Author & Business Philosopher

Chapter 4

Offering Outstanding Customer Service Equals Super Success On eBay

Chapter 4: Offering Outstanding...

154. Most sellers don't realise that it's not just about making a sale on eBay, it's about providing outstanding customer service before, during and after the sale has been made.

155. Go the extra mile by following up on your solution to a customer's challenge. Re-contact the customer to make certain that everything has been handled in a satisfactory manner and they are pleased with the outcome.

156. With so much competition, only premier customer service will set you apart from the rest, and all correspondence with your customer should start by telling them what you CAN do for them and not what you CAN'T.

157. Always make the tone of your email responses pleasant and helpful; remember the tone of your response can completely contradict your message, so be careful.

158. Completely review you customer's issues and address each one when you communicate back to them so they feel that you care and acknowledge how they're feeling.

159. When customers contact you, you're provided with a tremendous opportunity to reinforce and grow a relationship with them, so give them your all!

160. It makes sense to take the time and effort to make the communication between yourself and your customer as meaningful and service orientated as possible.

161. Attention to customer service will go a long way in helping you to satisfy your customers and make them feel special.
162. Always let your customers know in your email responses that they are a 'valued customer' and you hope to deal with them again soon!
163. Make sure that you use the buyer's name in email responses where possible and again in the subject line of any emails!
164. It's five times as hard to bring in new customers than it is to keep existing ones, so create a pleasant selling experience for everyone and you will see repeat customers.
165. Make your responses to your customers as personalised as possible; customers don't like it if everything is too automated, so make them feel special. It's no effort really and it pays off big time!
166. After answering questions, file them away in your folder so that you know you have responded to them already and you can systemise emailing your buyers in the future.
167. Always respond to your customers through eBay messages, not your personal email address. Be friendly and courteous and never send just one word emails like some silly sellers do; it's just too short and blunt.
168. Respond to answers quickly and thoroughly, as it keeps the buyer interested in your listing, and sets a precedent for what it will be like dealing with you after the sale is made.

169. Post responses to individual questions so others can see the answers and you won't have to keep answering the same questions.

170. Save time by answering buyer's questions quickly and easily with advanced FAQs and automated email responses.

171. See questions as money coming in and make them the first thing you do each day, the middle of the day and the last thing at night!!

172. Steer clear of using listing upgrades unless you have done your research and know for a fact that they will dramatically improve your end price.

173. The only listing upgrade we do recommend using each and every single time is the gallery photo, otherwise buyers will see the 'little green camera' in the search results.

174. Buyers don't have time to click on every listing and wait for the pictures to load, and if you don't display a gallery photo in the search results, you will lose sales.

175. Gallery Featured works along with the Best Match search filter can promote your listing 'above the line' in the special featured section above the general gallery items when buyers search for that particular product.

176. Currently starting at AU $19.95 for auctions and AU $59.95 for fixed price listing, Featured Plus would only be suitable for higher ticket items. Beware this upgrade as it can eat into your profits, so make sure you think it's worth using first.

177. To promote your listing further, eBay offers upgrades for your photos, and the fees will vary depending on the upgrade, the selling format that you choose, and the duration of the listing, so choose carefully!

178. You can choose a 'Basic Upgrade Pack' in eBay which combines a Gallery picture and an Item Subtitle for a discounted price.

179. With so many different options, the 'Value Pack' combines Gallery, Subtitle and Listing Designer to dress up your listing for prospective buyers.

180. There are also programs on the market, such as **www.auctiva.com** that charge you a minimal monthly fee to host your photos and create professional looking listings with templates.

181. Upgrades can be costly for smaller items that you're only selling from around the house for a few dollars; therefore upgrades are best used on more expensive items where you won't lose a lot of your profits.

182. Always write as much info in your listings as possible; include an accurate item description, Clear payment details, Postage and handling time, a simple return policy, your friendly terms and conditions, All specific product details, Item specifics and great photos!!! PHEW! This will ensure your customer knows as much as possible about the item up for grabs ;-)

183. I'd say that copywriting is the most important aspect of putting something up for sale on eBay. A good 90% of sellers have no idea of the power of 'storytelling' and the one area you can easily dominate, if you focus and follow proven strategies.

184. Knowing how to write a compelling, benefit driven description of your product will completely set you apart from the pack and could see you earning more money.

185. You need to write your 'product description', explaining in detail exactly what it is potential bidders will be bidding on. This way, you will eliminate many of the same repetitive questions.

186. The type of product you're selling, whether it's a household item or an expensive one-off collectable, will determine the amount of effort you put into the description.

187. Descriptions can be short or long copy, depending on the value of your item, as long as it's interesting!

188. You need to make your item descriptions compelling and full of benefits for potential buyers to have them wanting to buy your product.

189. Your listing description needs to be formatted so it's easy to read, rather than one long boring paragraph! Space the text and paragraphs out evenly and you can even insert photos to break the paragraphs up.

190. Think about your listing description like a piece of artwork… it needs to be easy on the eye and make your buyer want to buy!

191. Be accurate and cover all defects in your listing's description. Write as if there were no pictures so you leave no doubt in your buyer's mind about what they're getting.

192. Your listing and description copywriting skills might need a bit of practice when you first start out; however, as you progress you want to be able to hone them so well that you can sell ice to Eskimos, so to speak!

193. From our experience, the way you write your description will mean the difference between more or less sales and profits, so don't underestimate the power of a good description.

194. Never, ever blatantly copy someone's description of an item. You must write your own, otherwise your listing can be taken down by eBay. Not only that, but if you had bids already, they'll be notified by eBay that your listing has been pulled down.

195. Be careful if you're selling brand-name products, as eBay may want to see your proof of purchase to ensure you're buying from a licensed distributor.

196. When it comes to creating the text for your description, good grammar and spelling are essential if you want buyers to perceive you as professional and trustworthy.

197. Make the description exciting and informative, and tell the truth. If it's a once-worn pair of shoes, don't try to pass them off as new. Let's face it…shoppers aren't that silly!

198. Use compelling words like stunning, bold, or amazing to stir enthusiasm in the description body and provide plenty of detail. Give shoppers compelling reasons to bid on your items, rather than on other sellers' wares.

199. Provide as much information as you have about the item. Put yourself in the buyer's shoes. What would you want to know?

200. Also think about what type of market you're selling in. For example, if you're selling to a more mature market, you should have large easy to read text sizes and fonts. If it's too hard to read, they'll go elsewhere and you're likely to lose a sale.

201. Every store, whether it be retail or online, needs 'Terms and Conditions' so that customers and staff are fully aware of the business' set policies. If you don't have them stated clearly, you're leaving yourself wide open for problems and possible negative feedback.

202 No listing description is complete without a disclosure of your terms and conditions. Specify what forms of payment you accept. Include an estimate of shipping and handling charges, or better yet, provide a shipping calculator.

203. Your terms and conditions should state whether you will accept returns, and if so, under what conditions. For example, would you accept a return if the buyer is not 100% happy? What if the item turned up broken? Or they had a change of mind?

204. Your product guarantee should be very specific. Not being 100% happy, for instance, is too vague and by developing and publishing your sales terms and conditions upfront, your customers will immediately understand how you will manage the transaction from start to finish.

205. Make your policy easy to find by including it directly within your auction descriptions. Think the sale process through, covering all possible scenarios so you don't get caught later on.

206. Be reasonable with your Terms and Conditions; don't demand things like 'money orders only' or 'PayPal payment required - no exceptions'. Language like this will scare buyers away.

207. With so many millions of items up for sale every day, bidders have many choices, so if your terms and conditions are unfriendly, you'll lose the customer's interest fast and forever.

208. Don't charge obviously high handling fees with your postage; buyers will know and soon find another seller with more reasonable terms.

209. Similarly, customers don't respond well to restrictive shipping options, e.g. "I only ship once a week on Thursdays".

210. Be as clear as possible with your terms and conditions to avoid a barrage of email questions. If you still find you're getting a lot of queries about the item, you can always go back and edit your terms and conditions and include extra information.

211. Remember, you have the right to set your own terms and conditions, as long as they are within eBay's rules. Establish a standard policy that you can use with every listing and then stick with it.

212. By accepting as many payment methods as you can, you'll have a better chance of blowing your competition out of the water! The more you give… the more you get!

213. The more open-minded and flexible you are in business when it comes to servicing your customers' wants and needs, the more money you will make. It's up to you.

214. Don't miss out on a sale because you don't want to accept some payment methods, or you can't be bothered waiting for a payment to clear. Every buyer will have different methods they want to use to pay for items. As a business owner, you need to be able to accommodate every different method where possible.

215. In order to sell on eBay, you must accept PayPal as a form of payment. This was introduced as a way of ensuring that all buyers always had a safe, secure method to pay for their items.

216. PayPal is widely recognised as one of the safest and most secure methods of sending and accepting payment. You can increase confidence in your potential buyers by letting them see that you not only accept PayPal, but prefer PayPal payments.

217. Dodgy sellers have been known to strongly ask for bank deposit, because the buyer isn't covered by PayPal's buyer protection. They also want to avoid PayPal's fees.

218. PayPal is owned by eBay, so it's a smart idea to sign up for it as soon as you can. Some people don't like PayPal because it comes with fees; however, the majority of your customers prefer to pay via PayPal than any other way.

219. It's super important to think like 'a customer' and not about what you want. The easier you make it for your customers to pay, the more money you will make. It's a fact.

220. It's a good idea to offer as many payment methods as physically possible so there's no reason why buyers can't or won't shop with you.

221. Another bonus to offering PayPal as a payment method is that you will be able to accept all major credit cards through PayPal, which means buyers have the choice to pay for their purchases with available PayPal funds, or they can top up their account from their bank account or credit card.

222. Offering PayPal to international buyers is strongly recommended, as it's the most secure online merchant facility, and that will encourage more buyers.

223. If you're selling internationally, PayPal will also work out the currency conversions for you, which means you won't get stung with costly bank conversion fees and charges.

224. Don't limit yourself to selling within Australia only or you'll be denying yourself sales and profits!

225. PayPal is supported in 190 countries and regions, and posting worldwide will give you global exposure and higher sales volume.

226. Another payment method to consider, depending upon what you're selling, is 'Escrow'. Escrow is a third party service that 'holds' the payment on the buyer's behalf for financial security reasons. Using this service would be best suited for high-ticket items and products that need authenticating.

227. How Escrow works: Once you sell the item, the buyer pays the Escrow company and they then notify you, the seller, to ship the goods to the buyer. Once the buyer receives the goods and notifies Escrow they're happy with the goods, the funds are then released to the seller.

228. On eBay, Escrow services are most commonly used for expensive items such as Jewellery, collectibles and Cars and can bring you higher end prices, as the buyer has a chance to investigate the goods, prove they're genuine and authentic before finalising the sale.

229. Every year billions of dollars are lost due to Escrow scams, so only use an escrow service that eBay recommends, which are **www.escrow.com.au** or **www.escrow.com** as these are both registered companies.

230. Posting internationally doesn't have to be a confusing task; simply visit your local post office and get an international price list.

231. Always get insurance for sending packages internationally and most carriers will provide this service for you.

232. All your international packages must clear customs in the buyer's country, so make sure you are familiar with what paperwork you need to fill out.

233. Keep in mind that you can't just post anything and everything, the post office does have a list of prohibited items that you need to know about if you intend on expanding your business worldwide, which is a super idea!

234. There are several ways to send items internationally: Air Mail, Economy and Sea and depending on the value of your item and the time in which you want it to arrive.

235. Australia Post also has an international postage calculator on their website; check it out for accurate postage prices so you don't underestimate the cost. There's nothing worse than losing your profits to postage miscalculations!

236. By using 'item specifics' when listing internationally, the information will be translated into site languages for each country. This will help international buyers.

237. Selling internationally is just as easy as ticking the 'I will ship internationally' button, or if you prefer, you can just tick each particular country you want to sell to.

238. Remember that listing on different eBay websites may result in being charged different listing fees; make sure you find out exactly what you're going to be charged before listing on the other eBay websites.

239. If you list on your country's homepage and ship internationally, the currency will stay in your country's currency, making it easier for you. When a buyer views your item, they will see your currency and also what the conversion would be to their currency.

240. It's also essential to have a good pair of scales so you can weigh your items before quoting on postage. We started out with the good old bathroom scale before realising we needed to upgrade to become more accurate! *(Can you believe I used to stand on them holding the items and then subtract my body weight to get the package weight, as the bathroom scale couldn't detect such light objects? How funny!)*

241. Remember to allow for the bag, any packing material and sticky tape, etc., when weighing items and calculating costs.

242. Most sellers will get caught out underestimating the postage prices at one stage or another because most couriers and post carriers charge you for the 'cubic' weight of the item, rather than just the actual dead weight. This means the cubed space the item takes up rather than pricing based on the weight alone.

243. As a seller, you should never guess how much postage will be. There's a plethora of information available that you can educate yourself with, including booklets from the Post Office, online services and calculators that will ensure you'll never get caught out.

244. Remember to keep your postage costs as low as possible to encourage bidding. Buyers are also smart and will know if you're adding a handling fee on top of the postage price, which can affect your sales.

245. Whilst it's important to cover your costs for postage, packing products such as bags, boxes, bubble wrap and sticky tape, it's imperative that you keep these costs to a minimum.

246. Hot Tip: Check out the 'bulk' posting and packaging products available on eBay! You can also ask your local Post Office for bulk discounts, such as currently purchasing 100 tough bags at a time for a massive 65% off the regular price! How good's that?!

247. It's up to you how streamline you run your eBay business with postage and packaging costs, and it's vital to find a happy medium. If you're frivolous with your overheads, you can end up eating into your profit margins; however if you're too frugal on the other hand, using recycled bags and used packaging, your feedback may be affected.

248. When a buyer leaves you positive feedback, they also have the opportunity to rate certain aspects of your sale. These ratings are called the Detailed Seller Ratings.

249. Feedback ratings on individual aspects of your service dramatically affect you as a seller; therefore it's crucial to keep your costs to a minimum to avoid your ratings going down.

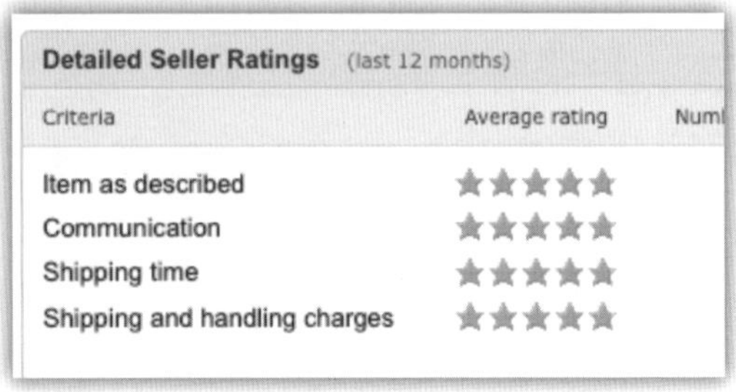

250. Another way to protect your feedback rating is to always ship your items in a timely manner; there's nothing worse for a buyer than waiting weeks for their new 'present' to arrive in the post.

251. Bear in mind that you should also explain the entire shipping process to your buyer, including how long the item will take to be shipped to your customer and include exactly what service you will be using for the postage. For example: do you offer regular, express or registered post?

252. First impressions count when it comes to packaging. Keep your packaging neat and professional because customers love receiving a well-packaged item. Depending on the value of your item, you can even tissue wrap or gift wrap the item for presentation.

253. It's a great idea to offer a tracking number on all of your medium and high-ticket items that you ship, so that your customers can track their item every step of the way. This will make them feel more comfortable about their purchase and guarantee your items don't get lost in the mail.

254. If any challenges do arise with your shipping service, act in a prompt and professional manner and assure your buyer you'll do whatever possible to satisfy their query.

255. Once you get your business on track, there's no doubt you'll eventually get a dispute from an unhappy customer. To avoid disputes on eBay, make sure your buyers get what they paid for. Don't misguide them in anyway and go out of your way to handle any disputes professionally.

256. If a buyer doesn't pay for an item you've sold them, you can try talking to them by phone or email. Most problems can be resolved through communicating directly with your buyer and you can request their phone number through the 'Advanced Search'.

257. If it's been a couple of days since your customer has won an item but not paid, try sending an email or giving them a quick call to remind them about payment; lots of people just get busy in life and might have forgotten.

258. An unpaid item dispute can be opened against a buyer if they have not made payment. This can be done after four days of the sale date; however, if you state that you give buyers seven days before payment is due then you need to give them that time.

259. An unpaid item dispute can also be opened if you and the buyer mutually agree to cancel the transaction for a number of reasons. For example, perhaps you lost or damaged the item and it was no longer available. Maybe the buyer made an honest mistake.

260. Unpaid item disputes are a great way to get your 'Final Value Fees' back and you may also be eligible for a credit on the 'Insertion Fees' after you re-list the item.

261. Don't forget if a buyer doesn't pay for your item, you can always send a second chance offer to another bidder, rather than miss out on the sale all together!

262. When you close an unpaid item dispute, the trust and safety team at eBay will automatically be alerted and actions may include recording unpaid item strikes on the buyers account. Too many strikes can lead to restrictions and/or suspension.

263. Whenever you list an item on eBay, you'll be charged an 'Insertion Fee' and the amount you get charged will depend on the type of listing format you use and the amount you start the listing at.

264. Low starting prices will encourage more bidding on your items from buyers and reduce your fees, so if possible, start your listing off as LOW as you're prepared to take for it and make sure you always round down your starting prices. For example, $19.95 instead of $20.00!

265. After the item has sold, you're also charged a 'Final Value Fee' based on the sale price. Click on this link to find out more about the Insertion Fees or Final Value fees: **http://help.ebay.com.au/Help/Selling/Fees**

266. For items listed in two categories, the final value fee is based on the fee schedule for the primary category, regardless of what category the item sells within.

267. If a buyer does not pay for their item by the due date specified in your terms and conditions, you can open an 'unpaid item dispute' so that you can claim back your final value fees.

268. If you have items that aren't in massive demand, you can even do a 'bulk listing' to save on listing fees. It may be much better to sell three books together for $9.95 instead of three separate listings at $3.95 each and three separate lots of listing fees. You can save on listing fees and your buyer can save on postage!

269. eBay often has promotions where they have reduced 'listing fees' or free 'insertion fees', so keep an eye out for the emails so you can make the most of the savings.

270. Thinking about how you're going to 'service' your customers before you get cracking is extremely important. Unfortunately, the majority of sellers on eBay are not serious business people and a lot of them lack great customer service. If you go out of your way to give outstanding customer service with a smile… you'll already be way ahead of the pack. Outstanding customer

service isn't something that just happens. It's planned and executed with the utmost importance.

271. If you want to enjoy amazing results with your eBay business, then you simply must give outstanding customer service and make sure you stand head and shoulders above your competitors.

272. The feedback system is the backbone of the eBay platform where your customer service will either see you shine or see you fail miserably. If you build a great eBay business and follow all the necessary success steps, your customers will buy from you again and again.

273. Many a successful eBay business is the result of 'word of mouth', which naturally comes from superior customer service, so go out of your way to help your buyers wherever possible. Make sure you answer all questions in a timely and polite manner.

274. Only speak in friendly tones… that's either on the phone or in the writing of your listings! You'd be bowled over at the rudeness of some eBay sellers.

275. Don't overcharge your customers on product or shipping fees. They trust you to do the right thing so take this seriously. Not only that, too much negative feedback brought on by this sort of practice could get you suspended!

276. Good customer service means making it as easy as possible for buyers to buy from you without hassles and delays.

Put yourself in your customer's shoes and ask yourself this question…"Would I let one of my family members buy from my eBay business?" If the answer is yes… keep on keeping on and if the answer is no, then change things and fast!

277. Your customers are paramount to your eBay success and even though they don't physically come into your business, treat them as if they did.

278. If one of your customers has a bad shopping experience with you, chances are they will tell around fifteen others... these people may have bought from you otherwise.

279. If your customers have a super shopping experience with you, they will share this experience with friends and family, and you'll probably get more sales as a result.

280. Why not give your customers a shopping experience to remember? Go all out to give them service or bonuses they won't forget in a long time.

281. Without customers, there is no business. They are the 'life blood' of your business, so treat them with the respect they deserve. Whether your customers spend $1.00 or $1000, they deserve nothing but the best customer service because you never know when they'll be back for more great buys!

282. Keep your customers updated with all the latest and greatest you have on offer in your eBay business. Why not offer extra bonuses so that buyers will choose you over your competition? After all, many sellers sell the exact same items, so what's going to make you stand out?

283. Win your customers' loyalty by making sure you continually grow and develop your line of products, and if you don't know what your customers want, why not ask them?

284. Ensure you let your customers know as soon as the item has been shipped… your customers will love you for it!

285. Make sure your customers know what's happening with their purchase every step of the way so that they don't panic and get 'buyer's remorse.'

286. What about offering your VIP customers a special newsletter with relevant information once a month? The better customer service you give… the more money you will make.

Bill & Irina Are Making $1,600 A Month Selling Their Friend's Unwanted Things On eBay

After implementing all the eBay steps **we learned from Matt & Amanda, we made $1,700 in the first three weeks** Now we're making $1,600 every month selling our friends unwanted items. We're looking at expanding and getting our sales up to **$10,000 a month** following the eBay Magic system and with the strategies we have in place this should happen within 6 months.

Thank you Matt & Amanda.

Bill & Irina Webster
Sydney, Australia.

"The real source of wealth and capital in this new era is not material things. It is the human mind, the human spirit, the human imagination and our ability to take massive action and our faith in the future."

Darren J Stephens
International Bestselling Author & Speaker

Chapter 5

What Happens After You've Sold Everything Not Nailed Down?

Chapter 5: What Happens After You've Sold....

287. Once you run out of things to sell from around the house *(and you've raided stuff from everyone you know)*, it's time to start thinking about what you're going to sell on an ongoing basis.

288. When deciding what to sell on eBay long-term there are two main areas you can get started:

    1. Check out the 'Completed Listings' where you can see exactly what's selling and what's not.

    2. Check out the amazing research tool…Terapeak. *Please note, there is a monthly or yearly cost involved with this search tool, however, for the information given, it's cheap as chips!* **http://tinyurl.com/BiddingBuzzTerapeak**

289. The 'Terapeak' research tool, which coincides with eBay's 'completed listings', give you so much more information than simply browsing the Completed Listings. You'll be amazed at what information is available at your fingertips and it's an absolute *must have* research tool for a successful eBay business.

290. It's *the* biggest question on everyone's lips: "What do I sell, and where do I get it?" Well, once you know how to read the stats in 'Terapeak', you'll never be left wondering what to sell on eBay again!

291. By using the 'Terapeak' research tool, you'll be able to see the demand a product has, how much supply there is, how often it sells, what time it sells best at and much, much more. It's a priceless tool if used correctly and, to tell you the truth, we couldn't run our eBay business without it.

292. As you're conducting your research on eBay for ideas on what's hot, make sure you take a good look at what other sellers are doing in the categories you're interested in.

293. When we were doing our research, we would keep a big book and write down all the things we liked about certain sellers and things we thought we could improve on if we decided to sell similar items. It's vital to know what you're competition is up to!

294. During the early stages, it's important that you gain momentum quickly so that you start to make a consistent income. The beautiful thing about eBay is you can start making money virtually right away, which in turn get's you so excited that you'll be busting to sell everything! *(Well we were anyway! ;-)*

295. Building a sustainable, long-term and profitable eBay business is like building a high rise. Step by step. Most of your efforts go into building the 'foundation' where you see the least amount of results. However, once you've completed this part properly, the rest seems to take care of itself and before you know it, the rewards are pouring in and there is less effort needed on a daily basis.

296. When we first started our eBay business, some of our well-meaning family and friends would laugh at us and say things like, "Don't worry; if your *little eBay business* fails, you can always go back to your old life."

Ever had *this* experience? Yeah well, it only added to our determination to be so successful that they'd all want our secrets! Stuff *that!* We've saved them for *you* instead ;)

297. Hot Tip: A lesson we learnt in the early days of having a business was *never* chase someone else's dreams. Eventually it will steal a little piece of your soul every day till you feel empty inside. You only get one crack at life… chase your own dreams and don't seek permission to do so. Dare to have it all.

298. The reason most sellers on eBay fail is because they are not educated when it comes to making real money on eBay and secondly because they don't know how to gain momentum. Most people simply jump from one 'bright shiny object' to the next and never get traction with one thing. If you stick to the proven system though, it will work for you. We are living proof to this day.

299. Self-belief is the real key to success in any business, including making money on eBay. If you think you can, you will… if you think you can't, you're already beat.

300. Some people see eBay as a flooded market where there's nothing left to sell, when in fact the super successful sellers see eBay as an untapped, golden opportunity to make unlimited streams of cash flow every day. Which category do you fall into?

301. If you're thinking about starting your own eBay business, it is wise to follow step-by-step proven systems to avoid painful, costly mistakes. However… only take the advice from those who have the results you want, as others are just not qualified.

302. Researching your business ideas before you start is a must when it comes to selling on eBay if you're serious about making money. Researching your markets and products expertly is a sure fire way to know if you're on the right track or not and will literally save you hours of frustration and heartache once you get going!

303. Make sure you have researched all your items thoroughly on
Terapeak, as this will help you find "hot" and "in demand" products that will sell instead of paying to list items that no one wants.

304. Hot tip: Don't panic and feel you need to stumble on a hot product right away. Building on-going streams of income takes patience, dedication and plenty of research!

305. It took us more than 6 weeks to find the category we wanted to sell in. We still sell in this category after nearly 4 years amongst others.

306. Having a long-term and profitable eBay business means sourcing products to sell continually so that you never run out. The trick here is to focus on building relationships with suppliers so that as you grow and become known, they will come to you instead of you going to them.

307. Knowing where to find legitimate long-term suppliers will depend on what style of eBay business model you set up. What you want to achieve from having it will determine how and where you end up sourcing your products long term.

308. If you want to set up a sustainable, automated eBay business, you will need to think about sourcing suppliers that can supply you ongoing. And of course, it may be a number of them, as you wouldn't want to put all your eggs into one basket. It's too risky.

309. You may have heard the saying 'your life goes in the direction of your most prominent thoughts.' Getting the right mindset and thinking long term is absolutely paramount if you want to enjoy success on any level. Here are some tips to help steer you in the right direction.

310. From the beginning, we had an idea of how much money we wanted to make, how many hours we wanted to work and what we were prepared to do to make it happen. We don't know what you want; however, take some time to think it through because what you focus on you attract.

311. Within 6 months of starting our eBay business our monthly sales had reached $50,000 and it took less than 10 hours a week to run it. It was 90% automated. Our dream business. We still run this business today and love it as much as we did from the start! *Your* dream business could be completely different than ours, so make sure you're clear from the start and remember…don't chase anyone's dream but your own.

312. Depending on how much money you want to make, how many hours you're prepared to put in and what you're prepared to do for it, the answers will ultimately have an impact on what products you sell on eBay. Remember… it's about having choices in life, not how much money you can rake in!

313. Did you know Antiques and Collectables is the most searched category on eBay today? Who do you know who may be able to supply you with this stuff? Or maybe you could visit some dealers and set up a 'consignment' deal? Who knows!

314. Here's one of our golden eBay rules. Don't get fixated on selling what you want to sell. Sell what people want and if you can't get your hands on your first choice of product, don't get all disappointed, move on to the next idea. Time is of the essence here and there is no room for emotion in this game!

315. Understand eBay can be a volatile market. You'll have your great days and not so great days, as with any business. However here's some comforting news for you… there's nothing that you will experience with your eBay business that we don't on a daily basis or haven't done over the past years. There are many, many others who have blazed the trail before you and now enjoy the eBay lifestyle and

freedom most only dream of. All you need to do is stay focused and open-minded!

316. 'Want It Now' – Did you know there is a specific place on eBay that enables buyers to let sellers know what they are looking for, allowing sellers to respond to buyers with eBay listings?... This can help you as a seller to expand your market and find more buyers.

317. Go to 'eBay Pulse' to find out what your potential buyers are looking for. You'll find it on the 'site map'. Here's one of our favourite haunts. It's where all the action is and where you'll discover what buyers are searching for on eBay! You can see what the top searches are for all categories on eBay and once you know how to use these tools, you're mind will expand beyond belief and you'll never go back. Guaranteed.

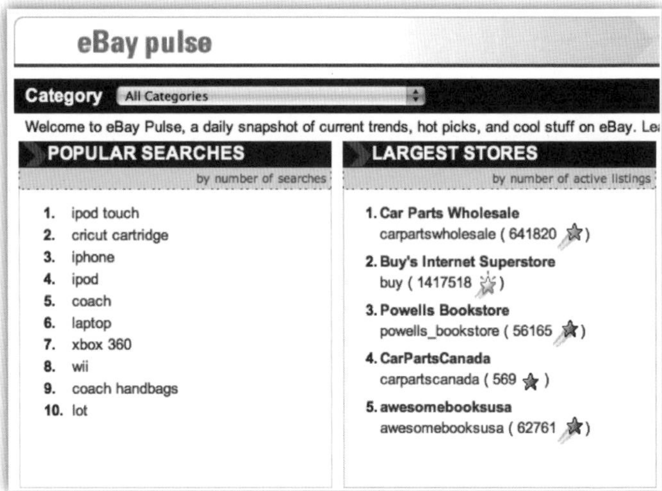

318. If you've been in business in the past for yourself, you're probably aware of the importance of systems and schedules. Without a schedule, you won't get the most out of your time and will feel like a 'little rat on the wheel' going nowhere fast. Yuk.

319. The importance of keeping a schedule can't be stressed enough. Have you ever gone to bed after a day of slogging away at your eBay Business only to remember you forgot to do something? Or woken in the morning with dread of all the things that you have to do today? Keeping a schedule means that you can work smarter and not harder, putting in the least amount of effort for maximum results.

320. A schedule allows you to allocate time to specific tasks, it offers you the opportunity to prioritise and incorporate all your daily tasks around your eBay Business.

321. We even go to the extreme of writing a 'to do list' every afternoon ready for the next day so that we can get the most out of all that we do. We start with the hardest tasks first and work our way down to the smallest and easiest. We find this is an immense help to keeping us focused, on track and on schedule no matter how busy things get!

322. Having a schedule you can easily stick to means you can streamline your business so that each and every day you know what specific tasks need to be completed and there is immense power in recognising that all the tasks that you had set out for yourself that day have been accomplished. Oh what a great feeling!

323. Without a schedule, you may not be working to your full capacity, allowing small tasks to slip through the cracks and, as we all know, it's the little things that we forget that can create larger challenges down the track.

Silver Powerseller Within 6 Months That's $3,000 US Per Month

3 Months after plugging into the Bidding Buzz system I made it as a Bronze Powerseller and another 3 months after that, I made Silver Powerseller! I couldn't have done it without the hold-your-hand every step of the way training that eBay magic has given me.

As an I.T. guy I thought I was pretty switched on but when it came to selling, I was an absolute newbie.

Without the support of the whole team at Bidding Buzz I would not have achieved the results that I happily see every time I logon to eBay.

Thanks for everything Matt and Amanda!

Clint Marsden, Sydney

Your past has nothing to do with your future and you can make a decision in a split second to be, do and have anything you desire. It just takes focus ,the right mind-set and the right action.

Amanda Clarkson
International Bestselling Author & Speaker

"You become like the people you spend the most time with, so pay any price to be in the presence of extraordinary people."

Darren J Stephens
International Bestselling Author & Speaker

Chapter 6

Treat This As A Business And Your Results Will Speak For Themselves

Chapter 6: Treat This As A Business...

324. If you want suppliers and customers to see you as a professional business owner that want to deal with you, you must take your eBay business seriously and act professionally.

325. If you don't have a professional eBay store and aren't prepared to invest in your business, why would suppliers want to deal with you?
Don't underestimate the power of a professional looking business card and what it can do for you. A well-designed business card can make your company memorable.

326. Most printers can create business cards; however, you shouldn't be too shrewd with the costs here or potential contacts may see this as a reflection of your business.

327. Having business cards on hand to pass out to suppliers and possible prospects means that you'll have a better chance of being their first choice for future business deals.

328. It's a great idea to customise your business card, so put on your creative thinking cap and tailor it to suit the audience you plan on marketing to and the services you offer.

329. Put some thought into your business card, as first impressions last. A cheap flimsy card reflects back on you as a business and you should invest in a high quality glossy or matte finish to help you stand out amongst your competition.

330. Use both sides of the card to maximise the marketing space, with additional contact information, customer testimonials, special offers or coupons you may have.

331. Why not include a photo of yourself so you can build professional relationships, plus your contacts can put a face to the name.

332. Here's another great tip. If travelling overseas, it pays to have one side of your card done in English and the other side in the language of the country you are visiting. We did this and had a great response from potential suppliers who were really impressed that we had gone to the trouble.

333. Don't forget the basics. Whilst it may seem obvious, some people fail to list all necessary information on their business cards. The basic elements of a business card include name, title, company name and web address, and all contact information including fax number.

334. The font size and style also matters, because you want people to be able to read your card easily. Never use a small font and, whilst it's great to be creative, avoid using a fancy font that's hard to read.

335. Don't go overboard with your business cards. Whilst they're worth every cent, you don't have to break the bank to find decent printers. Also check the costs involved

for different quantities; quite often buying them in bulk will be more cost-effective.

336. Important tip: Not having business a plan is like getting in your car and driving with no destination in mind. If you have a plan of some sort, at least you have something to aim for.

337. As I've mentioned, it's easy to chase the next shiny object when it comes to making money, so having a clear plan will help keep you focused and in line with your values and outcomes.

338. We never get bogged down with business plans that are pages long and get forgotten once you put them in your filing cabinet. Here are our thoughts on this topic:

339. A one-page business plan is as good as you need in the early stages of your eBay business. Anything more will bog you down and probably scare you off!

340 A simple SWOT analysis is all we go with at this stage. SWOT stands for Strengths, Weaknesses, Opportunities and Threats. You need to know this info before you get started!

341. The most important part of your business plan is knowing your'exit strategy or outcome'. Always start with your'end' in mind so you avoid going off track and on to things that are not relevant.

342. What is it exactly that you want from having an eBay business? If you don't know what you want, then it's likely you won't be that successful, as you won't know what you're aiming for, right?

343. We believe a lot of eBay seller's ultimately fail because they don't stay focused on the reason they went into business in the first place.

344. It's common to go off track and lose focus if you can't see where you're going with your business. Our advice is to get a mentor or at least have a clear view of what you want your business to look like.

345. Plan for 3 months, 6 months and 12 months down the track because if you only have a long-term plan, you may lose focus early in the piece.

346. Short-term goals are great and will keep you focused and on track whilst you're working towards your long-term goals.

347. If you don't know what you want from your eBay business, ask your family to help you so they get involved too. Be careful who you take your advice from though… make sure they have your best interests at heart.

348. If you need advice with your business plan, remember… only ask the advice of someone who's been there and has a result you want 'cause no one else is qualified!

349. Too many people are willing to take advice from those who have never taken a single risk in their lives! *Why is that?*

350. When we got into eBay… we didn't ask the advice of our family, our accountant or solicitor. We found out who were the best sellers at eBay and asked them. Not only did we ask them for advice, we paid big money to learn their secrets and you can see now how it has paid off.

351. Your plan will change regularly; however, your outcome may not and, as *times are a changing* as they say, there's always opportunity so move with the times and take advantage where you can.

352. You wouldn't build your dream home without a plan so why would you build your dream life without one?

353. A business plan comes in handy when you face those who want to steal your dreams. Without your clear plan, you may crumble under pressure and forget why you went into this in the first place.

354. Another reason we love to plan is that there are so many styles of eBay businesses. Unless you have a plan, you'll be all over the place, not knowing which type is best for you and your

I am more excited than ever to become an Ebay Millionairess

I just wanted you to know the phone call Michael and I had with Matt on Tuesday was AWESOME.

He is like an Ebay God! The wealth of information and eye for detail he so passionately gave to us is fantastic!

I have done the juicy tips he told us to do and already the traffic and watches have magnified. I am more excited than ever to become an Ebay Millionairess in 2 maybe 3 years time!

So if you happen to be 'passing him in the halls' anytime soon, could you please say a huge Thank you from us!

Thanks

Best Regards
Michael & Anthea Jones

"The Formula for Success is….
Clarity>Certainty>Confidence>
Action = Success."

Darren J Stephens
International Bestselling Author & Speaker

Chapter 7

Finding A Selling Method That Suits Your Personality & Gives You What You Want…

Chapter 7: Finding A Selling Method...

355. Everyone has different dreams and desires, and you'll find that different types of eBay businesses are more appealing than others, so make sure you look at the different ways of making money on eBay and pick one that best suits you.

356. Did you know there are at least twelve different ways you can make money on eBay? The best part… there's something for *everyone*! Whether you want to go big, small or somewhere in the middle… you can tailor your eBay business to suit you, your lifestyle and your family.

357. Depending on what you want to achieve, you can create the lifestyle you want with an eBay business once you have the 'know how'. It all comes down to education and understanding *what* you're doing and *why* you're doing it. Makes sense really, doesn't it?

358. **eBay Hobbyist.** Here's where you sell on eBay for extra income on the side. Hobbyists usually sell anything and everything as they're outcome is to simply top up their current income or get some extra money coming in.

359. **Drop shipping.** This is where you get a list of products from a wholesaler, list your chosen items on eBay and sell them. You don't pay for the items until your buyers pay you. You make your profits from the difference of what it costs you and what you can sell it for. Great if you're starting out on a shoestring budget.

360. **Consignment.** Here's where you sell other peoples stuff for them, which means you don't pay for the stock upfront. Usually you sell it and once the buyer pays you, the consigner splits the profits, depending on your agreement. Fantastic business if you don't want to invest in your own stock.

361. **eBay Drop Off Store.** Here's where you have a real 'brick and mortar' style of business. People bring their merchandise to your store and you sell it for them. Once the buyer pays, you split the profits with the owner of the merchandise, depending on your agreement. This can be a costly venture, so make sure you do plenty of research before you go into something like this!

362. **eBay Arbitrage.** Here's where you buy all of your stock off eBay from sellers who know very little about how to sell for profit! You then resell the same item on eBay, but do it properly using all the tricks the top sellers know about so you make a profit.

363. Once you know what you're doing you can really snag some amazing bargains! We know people who at times make over a $1,000 a week doing this. You don't even have to leave the comfort of your lounge for this one!

364. **Buying Wholesale.** Here's where you source legitimate wholesalers who are happy to do business with eBayers! Be careful, you'll stumble across many middlemen in this game; however, one place you can rely on for the right contacts is a company called World Wide Brands. **http://tinyurl.com/OneSourceSuppliers**

365. 'One Source' is the only company whom eBay endorses for wholesalers. You will pay a once off fee for a lifetime membership; however, it's worth the while as we personally know how much effort the owners put into this business to help you! Here's a tip. It may take quite a few goes to snag a great deal with a wholesaler; however, it will be worth your while in the long run.

366. **Selling Overstock.** Here's where you can get stock in bulk if you know what you're doing. There are millions of businesses who for many different reasons end up with excess stock all year round.

367. Some of these reasons may be… seasonal sales, fashion fads, economy and constant new stock coming in. As a seller, you can approach these companies and help move the stock. A bit of effort upfront, but the rewards are there!

368. Many storeowners are not able (due to certain contract and rules) to sell their excess stock online, and so this can be a win-win for you and the store. You've got nothing to lose, so why not go out and strike up a deal?

369. **Importing.** Here's where you deal directly with the Manufacturers. You can buy in small quantities or bulk, depending on what you want to achieve and your budget. Before you go down this path however, make sure you know what you're doing and have a clear plan of your outcomes.

370. With Importing, you pay for your stock upfront. Depending on the stock you're ordering and the time of year, often there'll be up to a three month wait (if not longer), as your stock is being made from scratch. Most of the time you can get amazing prices by dealing with manufacturers direct and you can import from all over the world, like America, India, Indonesia, China, Australia, Taiwan, Europe and many more countries. We have been doing this for years and love it!

371. There are literally thousands of Trade Shows all around the world every year you can attend where you'll meet manufacturers. Go to Google and search 'Trade Show.'

372. **Sell Information Products**. Here's your chance to share some of your hard-earned knowledge with the rest of the world. People all over the world are hungry for information and are happy to pay for it! Even though you can't sell 'eBooks' on eBay anymore, you can certainly sell hard copy

versions! You can create CD's, DVD's and even real books. We do this and often make an extra $200-$300 a week. Not bad considering it's a sideline to our real eBay business.

373. Hot tip: Never underestimate the value of your knowledge and what others are willing to pay for it. What do you know that others would love to know? Maybe you have a hobby or a special interest that you could teach others? Get some ideas by looking at the completed listings on eBay.

374. **eBay Trading Assistant.** Here's where you sell other people's stuff for them and advertise your services directly through eBay for free!

375. **Traditional Business.** Maybe you already have a traditional business and have never thought of moving stock on eBay as well? We have helped many of our members do this and sometimes they wind up making more on eBay than they do in their brick and mortar business all week! Goes to show, you can't beat eBay for traffic!

376. **Sell your services.** No matter what your trade is, if you have a service to offer, you can use eBay as a lead generator, sell your services and find new clientele, and broaden your customer database.

377. Remember… credibility and feedback are even more important when selling a service on eBay than when selling a product. That's because when selling services you are selling 'You'.

378. Now that you can see there are so many ways to make money on eBay, it's time to think about which method may suit you best. Take some time out now and write up your thoughts so far. Of course you can tweak as you go, but this is the start of your plan.

379. We have many customers who are implementing more than one method and now have multiple streams of income day-in-day-out. What a way to go!

380. There are many people who have a hobby eBay business and make a very handsome income. That's the power of being able to sell worldwide through the many eBay platforms.

381. A lot of people start out with an eBay business that is their hobby, but soon realize it can be much more than that. You can literally make as much or as little income as you desire on eBay and work from the comfort of your home if that's what you want.

382. eBay is the perfect business for those of you who want a home-style business, have children or just want to top up your weekly income to cover extra expenses or that special occasion. What would you spend the extra cash on if you had an eBay business?

383. If you're not sure about which style of eBay business is right for you, why not start off small and build slowly? You'll soon see if you want to take this to a full-time income or be happy with the extra cash-flow it will give you.

384. We know many people who have an eBay 'hobby' business and still make in excess of $100,000 a year income... Often buying stock from garage sales and government auctions. I don't know about you, but I think this type of income for a hobby business is extremely attractive!

385. A hobby business is a business you run part-time on the side that brings in sporadic amounts of income. Hard to automate in most cases, however, this style of business can be very lucrative just the same.

386. Having a hobby business is the perfect top up to an income stream for a stay at home parent, student, or someone who simply wants more money at the end of the month, instead of more month at the end of the money! Know what we mean?

387. Most hobby eBay sellers sell a variety of products and don't necessarily rely on their eBay business as their main source of income.

388. The beautiful thing about being an 'eBay hobbyist' is that it's super simple to switch to full-time, serious income. You simply have to make the decision and take the necessary steps to do so.

389. The best thing about taking your eBay business to the next level and making it your primary income stream is that, over time, you can easily ramp things up to automate a lot of daily tasks and free up lots of your time to do other important things.

390. There's no right or wrong way when it comes to making money on eBay... just make sure you treat it like a business and aim to be in profit mode to give you the lifestyle you want.

391. Remember… it's vital to build up your feedback score so you can gain credibility and trust with your buyers. We never recommend jumping in and trying to sell high-ticket items upfront. This doesn't work in the long run… you need to build your business starting with low ticket items and grow it from there.

392. Without feedback not only will your buyers not want to spend good money with you, eBay themselves can also limit or restrict your selling account if they don't see you slowly introducing your cluster of products.

393. Never assume what people will or will not buy on eBay. Big mistake. You have no idea what's in the buyer's mind at the time so let the market tell you and take the guesswork out of it! We once sold a video and book set to a guy in Slovenia! We couldn't believe it… The postage alone was nearly $100. The guy must have really wanted it so I'm glad we had it for him ;-)

394. The number one rule for making money on eBay is… Sell what people want… Not what you want to sell them!

395. Never sit around wracking your brain for things to sell on eBay. Use your research tools like Terapeak, PLUS eBay's available information to give you the answers. You'll come up with ideas you'd have never thought of in a million

years! In fact, we have a little blue book with over 279 product ideas in it that we know would make instant money on eBay. We know this because we've done our research as you now will!

396. With close to 80,000 new products being manufactured annually, there really is enough for everyone! Have an abundant mindset and you'll never be in fear of running out of ideas.

397. Important tip! Don't close your mind to thinking you must sell in your own country! You can choose to sell practically all around the world and this is why eBay is such a powerful wealth vehicle. In the early days, we sold most of our stuff into the USA! Talk about exciting stuff. In fact, many of our customers we currently mentor sell products all over the world from the comfort of their home. A Perfect lifestyle, don't you think?

398. When dealing with legitimate wholesalers, it's common that they'll expect you to have a registered business name. If they don't, then they are not legitimate but what we call 'middlemen.'

399. Getting a business name is nothing to be afraid of and it's very easy for you to do. It lets potential suppliers know you are serious about your business and have set things up the right way. If you don't have a registered business, you may come across a middleman wholesaler and chances are they'll say you won't need a Tax ID number or be a

registered business. The problem with this is that they'll get the profit margins you were chasing, which won't leave much for you.

400. To gain an ABN or Tax ID, you need a real shopfront with a street address and phone number for your business. Many wholesalers and other suppliers won't work with you unless you have one and you should be cautious of the suppliers who don't require this.

401. A business address, even if it's a booth in a shopping mall - makes you look legitimate to wholesalers, who can be suspicious of online businesses.

402. Last but not least, you need a business bank account, which is an account that is separate from your personal account and that carries your business name. You might have to keep a minimum balance on hand or be required to pay a service charge each month, but once you have a business bank account, you can use it to build credibility with wholesalers, as they see you are a legitimate business.

403. When sourcing products to sell on eBay, keep an open mind and be willing to put in the necessary groundwork. There are many wholesalers who are happy to work with online business people; however, you may need to speak with a few before you get the 'Yes' you want. The extra effort will pay off, so it's well worth it.

404. Before you start contacting suppliers, make sure you've done plenty of research and write down lists of products you'd be interested in selling. Most importantly though, don't get attached to any particular product initially, because if you can't get your hands on the stock, you'll need to move on quickly to another product. And of course, it always helps if you have some sort of interest in what you sell.

405. You can visit local shopping centres, malls and flea markets to get ideas on current trends and what people are spending money on. This is all part of the research process and well worth investing time in.

406. Take a look at the tags and packaging on products you see to discover who is manufacturing the stuff you're interested in. The more information you gather…the more ideas and leads you'll come up with!

407. Why not visit your local newsagent. There you'll find an abundance of ideas you'd never have thought of sitting in your lounge! Check out the hobby section to get ideas on what people are into and spending money on. **Hot tip:** If there's a magazine dedicated to it there are people spending money on it!

408. Here's your chance to approach retailers who may love the idea of another stream of income with your expertise help. If you approach them with a "win-win" offer, chances are you will easily find retailers happy to supply you ongoing. Especially around Christmas times and midyear stock-,take times.

409. We once interviewed a key staff member from World Wide Brands, **http://tinyurl.com/OneSourceSuppliers** a company who lists legitimate wholesalers who are happy to do business with eBay sellers, and they offer over 8.2 million wholesale products. She shared that it sometimes took up to 60 calls with different suppliers before they got a single YES! Are you prepared to do this kind of groundwork?

410. Remember… finding reliable sources of stock is just like panning for gold. Be patient, keep searching and don't give up if you get frustrated… there's gold out there waiting for your discovery!

411. When you do start talking business with wholesalers, they'll want to know things like your current business address, land line numbers, how long you've been in business for, how much volume you expect to turn over each month, business and credit reference, etc. Don't panic, it's all normal; however, don't lie, just be honest and let them know how much volume you predict, you may be able to sell based on all your research. If you've done that part properly the rest is easy! Remember…this business is about creating relationships.

412. It's normal when dealing with suppliers in the early days that you don't get credit on your stock. You may have to pay up front till you begin to build trust and credibility as an online seller. Don't be offended by this… go with the flow and be grateful you've found a supplier who is happy to work with you.

413. Another way to source ongoing, reliable stock is by buying direct from the manufacturer. As a retailer, you would normally only buy from registered wholesalers. As an eBay seller, you have plenty of options to explore.

414. If you want to import 'no name brand' items from places like India, Indonesia, Malaysia, Hong Kong and China for instance, you can deal directly with manufacturers.

415. You cannot however buy legitimate 'name brand items' from these places. Even if you are *guaranteed* that they are authentic, don't be fooled because if you get caught with pirated brand name items, the penalties can be devastating both on eBay and legally. Don't be tempted to go there, no matter how good the deals seem to be.

416. Customs and eBay take counterfeit items very seriously. Not only does eBay have the authority to cancel your listings, they can also permanently suspend your account for selling counterfeit items. Customs may even deny clearing counterfeits, which means you won't ever see the product.

417. We deal a lot with suppliers in places like China and find that doing business over there can be both rewarding and frustrating at times. Buying direct from manufacturers does have its benefits, like control of stock, simple to automate and often no problems with ongoing supplies.

418. At times the downside to importing from these countries is the turn-around time… it can range from 30 days right up to three months or more to have an order manufactured from scratch and shipped over. Orders may even blow out by months depending on seasons and how busy the manufacturers are.

419. When importing, you'll also need to stay on top of things like the quality represented. Often our version of quality and the suppliers can differ, so you need to be really specific.

420. Everything is paid for in US dollars, so the amount of money needed upfront to invest needs to be planned for. The global economy and how it affects the dollar's value can affect the ultimate values of your products. It pays off to do your homework thoroughly before getting into this arena, as it can be a minefield if you don't know what you're doing.

421. When you do decide on what products you'd be interested in, don't just stop at one supplier. Look for a minimum of three in case something goes wrong with one of them. The last thing you want is your eBay business to run out of stock because your supplier let you down!

422. If you do decide to import, you don't have to buy massive quantities of stock; you can get small boxes right up to 40 foot containers!

423. Important note: If you want to import your stock so you have more control, make sure you have thought about storage issues and quantity of stock. Because it can take three months to get it in the first place, you will need to place your next orders well before you run out.

424. There's no point looking at larger items like kid's ride on toys if you're not prepared to invest in a storage facility to hold it all. Many people prefer to run their whole eBay business from the spare room at home, so think about what items you are researching and stick to what you are prepared to do for the long term.

425. When we first started importing, we hired one of those Self Storage sheds till we worked out if importing was right for us long term.

426. You won't want to get yourself into big, expensive long commercial leases right up front if you can help it. They can be a huge burden especially if you outgrow the space or decide on a new product you can store at home in your garage!

427. During our first two years of selling on eBay, we moved storage sheds three times (because of our fast growth) till we got the right one! We ended up buying our own from the profits we were making. It was a painful lesson… but who would have guessed we'd become so successful at selling on eBay?

428. People shopping on eBay do love to buy name brand products over non name brands. However, don't despair, you can make a great living selling non name brand items. Perhaps you could mix it up by selling a bit of both? This way you'll give your customers more choice, which will in turn grow your business.

429. Hot tip. When contacting and speaking with suppliers (especially wholesalers) remember your manners and speak as you'd like to be spoken to. You'll have far more chance of getting your foot in the door this way.

430. Don't think that you're the one doing the wholesaler a favour wanting to sell their stock. Most of them don't initially want to do business with small business people like eBay sellers; they want to move their stock in big quantities to retail outlets. This is an important lesson, so be grateful at every opportunity you get to do business with them.

431. It is very common that suppliers will not deal with you unless you have a 'storefront.' In other words, a real shop. This can be frustrating for you, however most of the time they don't understand online business and may feel you won't be able to move much volume. We have helped people around this issue; however, keep going and don't give up. You *will* find a way!

432. It's a smart idea to get samples of what you want to sell ongoing before you invest a heap of money into stock. Many wholesalers and manufacturers will want you to buy

up big, but before you do, inspect the items and make sure you are happy with the quality before you move ahead.

433. If you are going to import, you can either jump on a plane and go over and meet your manufacturer to see how your products are produced, or you can have some samples flown over. We'd never suggest you *hope for the best,* as you may not get what you thought you would.

434. It pays well to do your due diligence before you import products from other countries around the world. Even though time is of the essence, losing your money and confidence can and will be far more painful.

435. Expect competition in whatever market you decide to sell in on eBay. It's a fact of life, so get used to it. There are times when you may order your stock with minimal competition on eBay at the time, only to find that by the time your stuff arrives, so has a few other sellers who have had the same idea as you!

436. If another seller comes into the market at the same time as you, there's little you can do about it apart from be the best in your chosen category. There are many ways you can do this and there's a good chance you'll be able to dominate your niche once you know exactly what to do.

437. Usually when you buy from Wholesalers, they will supply you with 'stock images' of the products you'll be selling. Make sure you check out your competition on eBay, because if you all have the same photos, how will you stand out from the crowd? If it were us, we'd get some samples and take some of our own pictures!

438. Other ways you can get your stock is by using drop shippers. This is a great way to get started if you don't have much to invest in your own stock or don't want the hassle of shipping!

439. Drop shipping is very popular amongst eBay sellers; however be careful not to end up being one of hundreds of sellers selling the same stuff. Again, you may be given a CD containing all the stock images, but be careful you don't get lost amongst other sellers.

440. Profits for drop shipping can also be much lower than other forms of selling on eBay. This is because the drop shipper is doing most of the work. He's storing the goods, packing them up and shipping them to your customers.

441. One of the biggest downsides to drop shipping is the lack of control you have over the stock. If the drop shipper runs out and you've already sold the item, chances are you're going to really upset your customers and probably get negative feedback. This is the last thing you want for your eBay business!

442. During the peak season when lots of stuff is selling on eBay, (especially when it comes to drop shippers) they will send out on a first come first serve basis. Or for those who move large quantities of stock. If you're just a beginner learning the ropes selling a few things here and there, chances are it will be you who misses out when the stock runs low.

443. Another idea if you do like the sound of drop shipping, is to set up deals in your local area or deal directly with suppliers. We have many customers who do this in Australia and make amazing profits for their efforts!

444. You can also drop ship wholesale items that you purchase upfront from suppliers. One of our students does exactly this; they import stock from Hong Kong and have it shipped directly to a distributer who is happy to ship the items out for them daily. They pay a small fee for storage space but the great thing is, they don't have to worry about the stock running out as they control it! How great is that!

445. Other students that we mentor have also set up deals with local retail stores where they sell the stock on eBay and the retailers hold the stock and send it out once the sale has been made. This is a great joint venture idea as you, the eBay seller, can focus on what you do best and the retailer now has another stream of income they never had before you came along! Win-win all around.

446. You could do the same with Antique dealers. How often have you walked into an antique shop and the owner is sitting behind the counter nodding off from sheer boredom? Why not help them move their stock, let them package it up carefully and ship to your customers? What a deal for both of you!

447. How about choosing a certain category on eBay you'd like to sell into and then approaching friends, family and business owners to supply you just in that niche? If you do this right and bring in the profits for them and you, before you know it, you'll have people knocking your door down with supplies. The word really does get out you know!

448. Did you know there are over 4,000 trade shows in America every year you could attend to meet potential suppliers? Hard to fathom huh? What massive opportunity awaits you right now! Go on... go to Google and start your research!

449. If you get stuck for ideas on what to sell, remember 'Want it now'. This is an area where buyers go on eBay and type in things they are looking to buy. Go to the site map on eBay and you'll find it there. If you can get your hands on the stuff these buyers want, you could be well on your way to filling a need other sellers have overlooked?

450. Check out places on eBay like 'Most Popular Searches.' Again, your buyers are telling you what they want to buy. eBay is run on the 'supply vs. demand' principle. If the demand outstrips supply, you're certain to cash-in if you follow all the rules.

451. We have been approached by a couple of name brand retail businesses that had a lot of surplus stock, to see if we'd be interested in selling for them on eBay. You could do two things here. You could buy the stock from them direct at a discount rate and resell it on eBay, or they could hold the stock and, then once you sell it, split the profits. See, there

are many ways to approach this business depending on the amount of control you want.

452. Don't forget the power of creating your own information products. You'd be amazed at what people will pay for information if they want it!

453. Here's another idea, what about packing up an information brochure, CD or DVD with your current product line, along with tips and strategies related to your niche? This alone could mean the difference of buyers shopping with you or your competitors.

454. Making your own information products doesn't have to be an expensive, drawn out ordeal. Simply use a camcorder and make your own. People love the *home* touch version better anyway. Remember, it's the information that counts not how perfect it is.

455. One of our staff members has a great eBay business where once a week she goes to outlet stores and Op shops. She buys all name brand clothing both new and pre-loved. In fact, she gets most of her stock from just a few favourite stores. Too easy.

456. This staff member then sells it all on eBay for massive profits, using the same listing copy over and over. She always doubles her money, at least. There have been times when she has made between $600- $1000 a week! Get this… she works for us full time and only does this for a few hours on the weekends. What a great idea eh, and a great *second income stream* too!

457. Another staff member of ours who works full time imports items from Hong Kong and she has the goods flown in every few months or so. Her items are only small, so she's able to do this from home. Each morning she checks her sales, packages up her parcels and posts them on the way to our office. She makes up to $600 each week in profits. Her business is fairly automated so it only takes around ½ a day to run. Not bad wouldn't you agree?

458. We have been importing household products for nearly four years now. We have our own warehouse and our business is automated up to 90%. It takes our staff less than two hours a day to run our eBay business. We now have time for our bigger purpose in life, which is helping and inspiring people like you all over the world to become cash and time rich with eBay.

459. Another staff member of ours buys his products from eBay and resells them for great profits using the 'Arbitraging' selling method. He also sells odds and ends as he stumbles across them like big tin sheds that no-one wants. You'd be surprised at how much he can fetch for this stuff. Of course, he's had great teachers to show him the ropes.

460. Another hot idea. He approached a furniture business last week that was closing down and bought some amazing bargains he'll make great profits from. This could be something you'd like to focus on... businesses that are going out of business for one reason or another. Unfortunately, there's a never-ending supply of them!

461. Another staff member has two 'drop-shipping' eBay businesses running right now. He's become a power seller in both categories and makes around $500 profit a week for very little effort. A few hours a week in fact. What could *you* be doing with an extra $500 a week right now?

462. This reminds me… another student who came to one of our eBay Magic workshops, loved the idea of approaching stores that were closing down. The very next day, after returning home from the workshop, she approached a store, which was closing down. Not only did she get a deal to sell everything left in the store, the owner actually imported stuff from all over the world and let her know that he'd be willing to import anything she wanted.

    He would stock the goods in his warehouse while she looked after the eBay side of things and split the profits. She couldn't believe her luck or how easy it was to get the deal. We weren't the least bit surprised! There's a deal just around the corner every day of the week ;-)

463. We know a lady who lives in America who only sells antiques on eBay. She gets all of her stock from garage sales that she and her mum visit every Saturday. She says she makes around $100,000 a

year and most of it is pure profits. She knows her stuff when it comes to antiques and getting a bargain! She runs her business from home and judging from the pics I've seen, there's not an ounce of room in her house for anything else! I bet she's having a blast though!

464. We read a story just recently about two girls who started their eBay business, bought all of their stock from the outlet malls and in their first year did a whopping $350,000 in sales. I would imagine that profits would have been around the 30-40% mark. Now, if these girls can do this, do you feel that you could too? They were selling clothes for large, curvy ladies sizes 18-36. Notice how niched they were in their chosen market? Very smart indeed.

465. From our experience helping hundreds of people become cash and time rich on eBay, we have discovered that there is a never-ending supply of things to sell on eBay if you are just willing to get off your bum and make it happen. We say, get your 'eBay goggles' on and look around you. What could you be selling on eBay right now?

466. At a past eBay Magic workshop we recently had, a 14 year old boy turned up with this great big photo frame of different cars. During the event, he put his hand up and came on stage to share his eBay story of buying and selling cars on eBay with 350 eBay fans! He would buy them, fix them up and resell them for big profits. His dad shared with me that he got his first car for just $1 and sold it for $50. He has since built that up to over $1250 in only 6 months.

467. After being at this same event, one man was so inspired by that kid he went home, cleaned out his own kid's bedroom cupboards, sold all the toys they no longer played with on eBay and made a whopping $1,000 within his first couple of weeks. After that, his kids put a big"KEEP OUT OR ELSE"sign on their bedroom door. Fair enough we say, however, they did love're-investing'in new toys!

468. Another lady focused on selling pre-loved videos and DVDs and made $4,000 profit in her first 30 days! What could you be selling right now? Just go to your cupboards and grab something you no longer want or need…it's that simple!

469. The golden rule is to keep your mind open. Start small and grow as big as you dream. It's up to you as you're only limited by your own mind and you'd be amazed by how many opportunities come your way once you're in the right mind frame!

470. Before you know it, you will have your own story to share with us. Make sure you email us if you would like to share it and inspire many others who would love to do what you're now doing! The tip is we just might have a special gift for you if you do.

471. Remember we said to start off slow and steady? Well if you've never imported from overseas before, your first order should be some samples to test and measure the market. You need to make sure you aren't just ordering one sample from one supplier; get enough to sell the products for a week or so to get a more accurate result.

472. Don't put all your eggs in one basket and rely on one supplier, have a few samples sent over from a few suppliers. Sure it will cost a bit more upfront; however, you'll be surprised at the difference in quality, packaging, service, price, etc.

473. Don't be fooled into finding a suppliers that has the cheapest prices overseas, always check out your product before you pay $$$ for it, whether you fly to see the product being made or order a sample, cheapest definitely doesn't always mean good quality.

474. Most suppliers can afford to negotiate on the price when you're buying in bulk, however, keep in mind that if you negotiate too much on the price, the manufacturer will negotiate on the quality to make up for it.

475. A basic understanding of the country you're dealing with will get you a lot further in your relationships and negotiations with your suppliers. Find out the basic courtesies so you make friends easily and avoid creating any tensions.

476. Knowing your payment terms before ordering is a MUST. Think the process through and ask lots of questions that can cover you in any circumstance.

477. In our experience, you can negotiate your shipping services with your supplier for samples; they may send them via EMS (worldwide express mail service) or via a courier of their own choice.

478. Be prepared when shipping samples in from overseas to pay customs taxes for your items. This cost will depend on the value of the samples.

479. Setting up an overseas courier company account can help with getting samples quicker because you simply give your account number to the supplier.

480. Be extremely careful when giving your account details out, because the courier will probably use the most expensive and quickest method of transportation unless arranged prior.

481. Expect your sample prices to cost more than the regular price per item, even up to double the usual price. This is because the costs of making a one-off sample are more expensive than making a larger run of them.

482. If you aren't confident ordering samples and arranging the shipping yourself, you can always use an importing logistics company to do all the legwork for you for a fee.

483. Arbitraging items on eBay to resell is such a great way to source stock from the comfort of your home, and there's a program called 'Going Going Gone' that is amazing to find products to sell ongoing.

484. With 'Going Going Gone', you can search for items that have 5 hours or less left before the auction ends, items that will end that same day, specific keywords, categories or even locations.

485. 'Going Going Gone' offers you the opportunity to buy items that may have gone un-noticed and you can grab yourself a bargain or two to resell!

486. It's also a great area for you to find yourself some more ongoing products to sell. You could buy products in bulk and then break them up and sell them in either smaller lots or singularly.

487. Another great feature with eBay is that you can sort the search results to be more specific. For example, you may choose to search for items that have free postage, or are very close to your home for pick up, or search for the items with the lowest price including postage so that you grab a bargain.

488. Once you've done a search on specific items to Arbitrage, you can even save your searches for the future so eBay will actually email you when new products that meet your buying criteria are listed... this means eBay will actually find you products to sell without you having to even be online!

489. Running a successful Arbitrage business involves finding poorly listed items, then buying them for a low price and reselling them for a higher price.

490. You can also use online software tools to 'snipe' the bargains for you. This means you can find products from all over the world and don't need to wait up late to buy them.

491. You can Arbitrage items from other auction sites that don't have the traffic eBay does for a minimal price and resell

them on eBay, or find a never ending supply of products where sellers don't know what they're doing.

492. Look for listings that have no gallery photo, poor photos or bad lighting which makes it hard to make out what the item in the photo is. Items that don't have a good description or even sellers that have little to no feedback are also great items to keep an eye out for!

493. Another way to profit from inexperienced sellers is to search for items that have misspelled words in their titles, which means buyers can't find the listings.

494. Misspelled keywords in your title description can drastically reduce the amount of traffic diverted to your listing, so make sure you check your spelling!

The very first auction we ever put on eBay… we spelled the word Internet wrong, (We left the letter "R" out) however, lucky for us we still made money... but we might have made even more if we had of checked our spelling, right?

495. There are great tools out there such as **www.fatfingers.com** that will actually help you find misspelt words in the titles. When we did a search for "Ralph Lauren" in the US, a massive 823 sellers spelt the brand incorrectly... can you start to see the power of Arbitraging?!

Remember to always find out what's hot in Terapeak first so you know what to keep an eye out for when arbitraging. **http://tinyurl.com/BiddingBuzzTerapeak** *Don't forget there's a fee to use this program and well worth it I might add!*

496. You can also look for items that are in inappropriate categories and snap them up because again buyers may not find these items when they're listed in the wrong category.

497. eBay also allows you to save your favourite searches in eBay and then whenever someone lists that item with the title spelt incorrectly, you'll get an email letting you know!

498. Don't limit yourself to Arbitraging in your local country.... you can also buy and resell from other eBay platforms if there's a bigger demand in that country. Again using the power of different currencies on the open market.

499. Look for items where the seller obviously doesn't know the value of the item and is selling it below cost. You'd be very surprised how often this happens on eBay.

500. Many sellers neglect to spend time writing a description that sells their item and you can Arbitrage items that have bad descriptions and don't tell the customer what they need or want to know.

501. Stick to a product that you know about, or do your research so you make money from Arbitraging. We know quite a few people who make full time incomes using this one method only.

502. Arbitrage from other online auction sites such as…
www.oztion.com.au
www.gumtree.com.au
www.craigslist.com.au
You can buy from unlimited items to resell onto eBay. There's good money to made here if you know the values of items you've researched!

503. Look for items where sellers are not putting the brand name as one of the keywords in their title. It may seem pretty obvious, however many sellers don't realise that eBay is a search engine.

504. If you're unsure of what price items are selling for and if you want to make sure you're getting a bargain then check out'Completed Listings', which you'll find under the Site Map, to gauge prices that are ended.

505. Abbreviations are also a common mistake many sellers make in their titles, as they couldn't fit the full spelling in the 55 characters you have available in the title.

506. No matter what you're selling, it's a great idea to let the buyers know what the RRP (recommended retail price) in the listing is, so they know what it's worth.

507. You can search incorrectly spelt words not just by title, but also in the description, by doing an advanced search in eBay and ticking the 'Title and Description' box.

508. To search for *several* words in the search box for incorrect spelling, you just need to enter the keywords in parentheses and then separated by commas.

509. Remember to calculate any shipping costs into your final price when you're considering purchasing products to sell, because if the shipping is too high the products may not be viable to sell at a profit. This is especially important if you're considering importing your stock in from other countries.

510. If you find an item spelt incorrectly without any bids, place one immediately! Otherwise, if the seller realises they have misspelt a word or want to fix up their photos / description, etc., you may lose your opportunity to bid. Once a bid is placed, the seller won't be able to revise the item or make any changes.

511. You can also use a sniping tool to bid on your behalf in the very last few seconds of an auction so you don't have to be online! There are a few different ones you can choose.

512. Arbitraging is one of the quickest ways to find stock without leaving the comfort of your home and is a way to ensure you never run out of things to sell on eBay... so start arbitraging today!

513. Be realistic about where you start when you're approaching suppliers. If you have zero feedback and no business plan, chances are you won't be able to source well-known brands easily.

514. If you feel more comfortable dealing with local suppliers, then source your products locally... if you can get something in your own backyard, then why not? We have had many of our students do this with success.

515. Establish good relationships with your suppliers and don't be afraid to email or call with questions that you may have. After all, they're in business to make money too right?

516. If a supplier stops answering your questions, they are not someone that you want to do business with and may have something to hide. These types of suppliers always get the alarm bells ringing so be aware and make sure you stay in touch often.

517. Constant communication with your supplier will help them realise that you're serious about your business, and as time goes on, they'll often give you better terms, deals and freedom with your orders.

518. Buying items in bulk will mean you will often make a much higher profit margin per product.

519. It's great to sell something that you're interested in, however, don't get too focused on what *you* want to sell. It's imperative to sell what people want to buy. Give them what they want and you'll get what you want.;-)

520. If you have knowledge about collectables and antiques, then go to as many garage sales as you can because it can be an extremely rewarding adventure. You never know what treasures you'll find that can be turned into big money!

521. When targeting neighbourhoods for garage sales, one tip is to look for the more affluent areas where you could possibly find good quality items at bargain prices.

522. Check your capital city for Trade Fairs or Expo's, as they are a great place to source from and often have many interesting wholesalers ready to do business.

523. Always do your 'due diligence' with any supplier before placing an order with them. Find out as much information about their company as possible, and if you can, go and visit the factory and meet the people.

524. You'd be amazed at the treasures you can source from flea markets, car boot sales and garage sales once you have your 'eBay goggles' on. A good idea might be to buy only things that are in certain categories. This way, you won't come across as a 'junk yard' on eBay, which isn't your ideal business.

525. If 'drop shipping' is the way you want to go, make sure you focus on building a great relationship, as you want to make sure they send your items out on time so you get positive feedback from your buyers.

526. Estate Sales are full of great little treasures to buy and resell on eBay. Often you can buy 'bulk lots' in one go, rather than one-offs here and there.

527. Make sure if you're heading out to source items from garage sales that you get there earlier than everyone else to get the best deals and treasures! Get up early and plan your day to make the most of it. We have many students doing this and they're not only having fun, they're making great profits too!

528. Find out what time the garage sales are finishing so you can go back and offer them a bulk price for whatever's left. You'd be amazed at what bargains you can pick up!

529. More ways to find suppliers…you can check out the local Yellow Pages, as there are loads of wholesalers and manufacturers you can get in touch with.

530. Liquidation and overstock sites are great for sourcing products from *and* you can check them out online. Just make sure you do your homework and be prepared to get on the phone if necessary.

531. Research all suppliers before you buy anything from them because you must make sure they are reputable and have a good track record. Ask them the names of other businesses they supply to. Be prepared to call them, fax them and visit them to ensure they're legitimate.

532. Google is generally full of 'Middlemen' product sellers, however, it can be a great tool to help you locate local distributors and even manufacturers you can contact.

533. No matter where you find your supplier, ask them lots of questions until you feel comfortable dealing with them, including what payment methods they accept. After all, you may be doing business for many years to come!

534. Telegraphic Transfer is the most common payment method to pay overseas suppliers. It's also called T/T in short, so when you see this term on a supplier's website, it means technical or telegraphic transfer, i.e. from bank to bank.

535. From our experience, telegraphic transfer (sometimes called a wire transfer) is the simplest, cheapest and almost fastest method of sending money overseas.

536. Sending money overseas can incur fees which range from $15 to $30 per transfer and you should allow three to five working days for the cash to hit the foreign bank account.

537. Sending money through your bank isn't the only way to wire money; there are external companies that can help you transfer your money safely for a small fee. Of course, let's not forget you can also do this with PayPal.

538. When you send money overseas there may also be other fees charged by overseas banks, due to transfer costs of banking in that country, so you can use companies such **www.travelex.com** to avoid bank fees.

539. Many financial institutions offer reasonably up to date foreign currency information and some have foreign exchange calculators. Foreign exchange rates used with wire transfers can add to the cost, so get some quotes before committing to your bank of choice.

540. If you have internet banking set up, you can transfer the money yourself from home, however, check your limits first before trying to send money to a supplier.

541. A Letter of Credit also know as L/C is a well-known payment method for purchasing stock and is basically where the bank sends your supplier a letter of credit based on the value of your assets. Obviously, you need to apply for this with your bank and jump through a few hoops!

542. Even if your supplier does accept bank cheques for payment of your stock, it can take several weeks until they receive it and it clears, so it's a very long drawn out process. Time is always of the essence so I'd suggest doing this as a last resort.

543. Some suppliers will allow you to pay through PayPal for your stock, however, even though it's usually a safe payment method, there are quite high fees on the suppliers end.

544. I would strongly recommend NEVER giving out any credit card details over the phone or via email to pay for stock. Credit card fraud is very serious and real. Always use a safer payment method.

545. When paying suppliers overseas for products, make sure that you're always paying for the FOB price. This means 'Freight On Board' cost and this is the cost they charge you to pack the goods into a container and send it to their local port. If you don't allow for the FOB price and shipping, there could be hidden charges on the invoice.

546. 'Cash in advance' is a payment method that some suppliers may use, where you pay the supplier for your stock before shipment is made. In most cases, they won't release the stock without payment anyway.

547. It's normal for a manufacturer to require around 30% for the deposit to purchase the 'raw materials' needed to produce the goods and then the 70% balance when the goods are on the water.

548. 'Western Union' is a form of Electronic Funds Transfer System that allows you to transfer funds between individuals and businesses. This is mainly used when the two sides of the transactions are on different continents or areas of the world.

549. When it comes to eBay and paying suppliers, we recommend you always avoid paying Western Union for your imported goods. Western Union is a very unsecure payment method and is basically untraceable. If this is your supplier's only selling method.... run the other way!

550. From our experience, 'Western Union' money transfers are commonly used by unscrupulous 'middlemen' who will often take your money, never to be heard from again. It's the poor unsuspecting client that gets hurt in the end.

551. Western Union is one of the most frequently used money transfer services, so if you don't conduct your due diligence, you could experience financial loss. We know of many cases of this happening.

552. With Western Union, we've found that this is the most unsafe method of payment for goods and or services, as there is no real way of keeping tabs on where the money has gone and who it has gone to... it's just not secure enough to ensure a safe transaction.

553. If a supplier doesn't offer a range of payment methods, we would avoid them at all costs. Let's face it, as a seller would you only accept one payment method?

Travelex worldwide money

The world's foreign exchange company

I Was Blown Away With How Much I Learnt In That One Conversation

I would like to use this opportunity to say 'THANKYOU' for mentoring me in my ebay journey which started at the end of November 2009.

You have so professionally advised me, shared with me your expert knowledge and experience and supported me through times when I didn't know if I could get through the steep learning curves. I have so appreciated you responding to my emails so promptly. Your advice and suggestions, I have always taken to heart and with each step you lead me, I am so confident that you are teaching me well.

Thank you for your encouraging words which have spurred me on when I was feeling so frustrated.

Thank you for the phone appointment recently when you so very patiently went through the research process. I was blown away with how much I learnt in that one conversation. And then, you sent me an email which was loaded with more advice, direction and an open door for me to ask even more questions!!

I am very grateful to you and feel totally privileged to have you as my mentor. For that,I am more determined than ever to make my ebay business work.

Thank you!

With Best Wishes Elsa Arbuckle.

Here's Some Interesting And Fun Facts About eBay Worldwide...

554. The very first item sold on eBay was a broken laser pointer for US $14.83.

555. Founded in 1999, eBay.co.uk is the UK's number 1 ecommerce site, providing a platform for over 17,000,000 unique visitors per month (Nielsen / Net ratings, January 2010) to buy and sell new, unique and used items in a fun and easy way.

556. Sellers of all sizes, including 120,000 registered businesses and 20 high-street retailers use eBay.co.uk to reach the UK's largest online shopping audience.

557. In 2010, eBay Australia reached over 8,000,000 registered users.

558. During the 2009/2010 financial year, there were 106 people who did more than $1,000,000 turnover on eBay Australia.

559. The town of Bridgeville, California was sold on eBay.

560. eBay has a global presence in 39 markets, including Australia... just imagine the possibilities!

561. The most expensive item sold on eBay in Australia was a Ferrari F355 1999 Berlinetta F1 which sold for AU$151,100.

562. A toy is sold every 24 seconds on eBay Australia.
563. Every minute a mobile phone sells on eBay UK.
564. A piece of jewellery sells every 6 minutes on eBay India.
565. Over 30,000 NEW and USED clothing, footwear, & accessory items are sold every day on eBay.
566. A golf foursome with 2002 Master Champion Tiger Woods sold for $425,000.
567. A 50,000-year-old mammoth was put up for sale in 2004 with a minimum bid set at US $250,000 by his Dutch owner due to lack of space, and sold for £61,000.
568. UK shoppers account for approximately 64% of the items bought through the eBay app across Europe
569. Sellers of all sizes, including 120,000 registered businesses and 20 high-street retailers use eBay.co.uk to reach the UK's largest online shopping audience.
570. In the aftermath of both the 2004 Indian Ocean Tsunami and Hurricane Katrina, the Tonight Show auctioned off two

Harley-Davidson motorcycles which had been signed by various celebrities. The winning bid for the motorcycle auctioned after the Tsunami was $800,100.

571. eBayers' in the UK spend more money on eBay than they spend on going to the movies.

572. In 2004, a Seattle man posted pictures of himself wearing his ex-wife's wedding dress. In more than one way, the seller received much more than he expected. While he initially admitted he was selling the dress to earn some money for Mariners tickets, the bidding got into the thousands of dollars, and the seller actually received a number of marriage proposals from users.

573. A group of four men from Australia auctioned themselves to spend the weekend with the promise of "beers, snags, good conversation and a hell of a lot of laughs" for AU$1,300.

574. In June 2005, the wife of Tim Shaw, a British radio DJ on Kerrang! 105.2 sold Tim's Lotus sports car with a Buy It Now price of 50p. This was after Tim's wife heard him flirting with model Jodie Marsh on air. The car was sold within 5 minutes.

575. A CD sells every 11 seconds on eBay.

576. The most expensive item sold on eBay to date is a private business jet for $4.9 million.

We Now Ship Worldwide & Our Business Is Fully Automated. We Make Between $600 to $1,000 A Week

Matt & Amanda,

Hi, just wanted to let you know how happy we are with your course.

We have been members since Christmas, receiving your weekly lessons, and have built a successful eBay business.

We now shipping worldwide and our business is fully automated. We are now looking for a second niche. Using your research technique sand research tool we have a list of hot items to choose from.

We are saving up to order a larger shipment of a bigger ticker item.

Before starting your course we had never used eBay and we are now planning our new future around it.

You were right. It is very exciting to wake up every morning and look at our PayPal account to see how much money we made while we slept.

So thanks again, love the course.

Michael & Cherie

All that you achieve and all you fail to achieve is the direct result of your own thoughts…

James Allen

"The big secret in life is that there is no big secret. Whatever your goal, you can get there if you're willing to change your mindset, focus and work at it."

Darren J Stephens
International Bestselling Author & Speaker

Chapter 8

Taking The Leap of Faith After You Find Ongoing Products To Sell

Chapter 8: Taking The Leap of Faith...

577. With every selling method, you must plan all of the steps in the process for your eBay success. People don't plan to fail, they fail to plan.

578. Take time out of your business every week to 'think' things through and plan for future growth. We do this every Friday and it's had a massive impact on our business in a positive way.

579. When you're stressed out and tired of trying to run a business, often you'll make silly and costly mistakes, so take the time to think things through before you act, because from our experience you'll save yourself time, money and headaches if you do!

580. When making big decisions both financial and personal, we take a notepad and write down all the *pros and cons* of what will be the outcome of that decision, and whichever list is longer, we often go with that decision.

581. Never ask the advice from those who do not have what you want, or have not done what you want to do, because they're simply not qualified to give it. Always follow those who have blazed a trail you want to walk.

582. Stick to goals that are achievable and can be reached in a time frame that's not too far in the future. It's easy to reset your goals if you hit them and then keep raising the bar.

583. It's OK to dream big. We do every day and you'd be surprised at how many targets we reach that would have seemed almost impossible when we first set them!

584. Keep an open mind… you'll learn something new every day and grow a little more.

585. Concentrate and focus wholly on your goals and dreams. It's easy to let others distract us and even easier to let ourselves get distracted.

586. Avoid 'the next shiny object' once you've set your goals. You must stay 100% focused on your outcome and never lose sight of the prize if you want to taste success on any level.

587. Be careful who you share your goals and dreams with… there are dream stealers on every corner waiting to steal yours from you and make you feel silly for wanting all that you aim for!

588. Never go into business with anyone whose values and outcomes are not aligned to yours… the wheels will fall off your wagon sooner than later if you do.

589. There are many times you'll feel scared and alone on your journey to success. Never fear… you're not alone and all you need to know is that someone before you has walked the same path and made it.

590. Lack of enthusiasm will kill your success goals quicker than a speeding bullet. If you cannot get enthusiastic about your own goals… then why would someone else?

591. Success is measured on many levels. Why not set goals for all areas of your life?

592. Goals are your 'guiding light' to help you stay on track and focused on the reason you started out on your journey in the first place.

593. We set goals daily, weekly, monthly, yearly and five years down the track. Setting short-term and long-term goals gives us short-term pleasure and something to look forward too. If we only set the five-year goal... it would seem an eternity away!

594. As your business grows… so will your personal goals and it's OK to reassess your goals as often as you like, as long as you aim to keep moving forward in a positive way.

595. Every day we ask ourselves the following question. *'Is what I'm doing right now taking me closer to my outcome or further away from my outcome?'* We spend the majority of our time doing things that move us towards our goals.

596. Ask yourself the above question at least 5 times a day… you'll be amazed at how great we can be at avoiding being successful and doing tasks that aren't that important! Talk about self-sabotage!

597. Once you reach a certain goal… set another immediately. Life is about experiencing all there is to offer, so goals are never-ending if you want to make the most of it.

598. Don't beat yourself up if you don't reach a certain goal by a certain date. Re-focus and re-set the date. If you want it

badly enough and you take action every day, you'll get it. This we can guarantee.

599. Your goals must'make sense' to you. If you're chasing someone else's goals and dreams, it's not going to work, because you are not being true to your own values.

600. Also remember... if you want something different in life, you must do something differently, because what you've always done won't take you to where you want to go.

601. You don't have to take the long road to reach your goals and dreams; every top entrepreneur, sporting legend and successful person has had coaching and mentoring at some stage of their career.

602. Everyone needs a mentor in order to reach all the goals you set. Choose your mentors very carefully. Unfortunately, not all so- called mentors will have your best interests at heart.

603. True mentors will show you how and help you break your goals down into achievable tasks based on your needs, wants and desires.

604. Choose a mentor who has without doubt'walked a mile' in your shoes and has already blazed a trail. It will save you years of heartache and frustration.

605. When breaking your goals down, push yourself to do more than you normally would during a weekly period. We believe most people only do what they must to get by, therefore never really experience true wealth or success to the degree they'd really like.

606. Hoping, wishing, praying and putting it out there is NOT enough to see your goals come to fruition. The most important thing of all is taking massive action. Only then can you expect anything great to happen.

607. Every day we have a 'tick off' system to make sure we're on track with our daily goals. We start off with the hardest task and work our way down. Only when all things have a big red tick against them do we stop for the day! *(And reward ourselves with a delicious glass of red wine ;-)*

608. The reason we start the day with the hardest or most challenging tasks is because the mornings are where we're most energized and things seem easier! Not only that… the rest of the day seems like a breeze!

609. If your goals are not challenging in any way, you have set them too low and too easy. Setting *meaty* goals are meant to stretch your mind and personal comfort levels. If you're not stretching and learning every day, how can you expect to get a different result?

610. We get together at least once a day to discuss how we're doing with achieving the goals we've set. You don't have to do it every day, however at least once a week is a must to stay on track and keep focused.

611. If you find you cannot stay focused on your goals, then write up one hundred reasons why your goals are important to you in the first place. This will tell you if you've set the right goals or not.

612. Unless your goals and dreams are part of your being, it won't be easy to stay on track. Everything else that's unimportant will soon get in the way.

613. Once your goals are broken down into easy to deal with chunks, you'll quickly and easily see where you might want to make changes. We do this all the time, however, our 'end picture' never really changes.

614. Because you cannot control outside forces, when it comes to business and goal setting, you must be able to adapt and change with the times and keep your emotions intact.

615. Remember… one step at a time. Make sure you leave time for other important things in your life like family and play time. It's a challenge balancing work and play, but an absolute must for long-term success!

616. It's also normal to get 'cold feet' and procrastinate when chasing your goals and dreams in business and life. Remember… someone else has usually already been there before you and lived to tell the tale…

"How Serious Are You About Your Success?"

617. You must have unwavering courage and keep your mind focused on all the reasons why you wanted to experience success in the first place.

618. It takes courage to go out and achieve all you desire out of life, but it takes *no* guts to be average and live a life of quiet desperation.

619. Avoiding cold feet and procrastination requires self-control in the beginning. Although you'll often feel scared and uncertain about your future along your journey, you'll soon get used to making the hard decisions, based on what's going to take you closer to your outcome rather than further away.

620. Once you have made the decision to become successful in your business and personal life, this will be the very reason you'll keep going when you feel uncertain and scared about your future.

621. Here's one of our favourite sayings..."I'd rather go through life *knowing* than end my days *wondering*". You deserve to be abundant, now go and make it happen!

622. People who never accumulate real wealth on all levels are too eager to listen to other people's opinions and those who don't have any real results. If you don't want to fall into this category, then keep moving forward every moment of every day... you'll see that it can all be worthwhile.

623. No one will ever care about your goals and dreams as much as you do, so don't expect anyone else to work at getting them as hard as you should.

624. *Fear, procrastination, cold feet...* call it what you will. It destroys determination, action, and your chances of achieving success. Get around others who are successful and on the same path as you and your chances of failure decline rapidly.

625. Look in the mirror and say nice things to yourself everyday, because there're plenty of others out there who are waiting to pull you down any chance they get. Every day I look in the mirror and tell myself how smart I am and how there are thousands of people out there waiting for my words of inspiration. What do *you* say to *yourself*?

626. Another way to avoid procrastination is to mind your 'language.' Speak in a positive tone rather than a negative one, because you become your words, so to speak.

627. You must believe in yourself 100% before you can expect anyone else to believe in you too, so be kind to yourself and tell yourself every day that you deserve success in business and life.

628. As Tony Robbins says, 'You've got two things in life... results or a story as to why it didn't work for you'. It's your choice so don't let procrastination and fear hold you back one more second! Are you going to let your old story go and make your goals a reality?

629. The quality of your mentor and teachers will determine the quality of your knowledge and education...

   The quality of your education and knowledge will determine the quality of your beliefs and dreams...The quality of your beliefs and dreams will determine the quality of the questions you ask...

   The quality of the questions you ask will determine the quality of the decisions you make in your life...The decisions you make in your life will determine the quality of actions you take as a result...

The quality of the actions you take will determine the quality of results you experience on all levels...The quality of results you achieve will determine the quality of life you live...

"Success Is a Choice...And So Is Failure... What Will You Choose?"

630. Avoid procrastination by sharing your goals with those you trust. By putting it out there through speech, certainty and belief, this will in turn motivate you to take action and maintain it.

631. If your *dreams* are big enough... the *how* is easy. Make your reasons and dreams so important that there is no other choice than success. In other words, burn your bridges.

632. By the time you're seventeen years old, you've heard the words 'No you can't' an average of 150,000 times. And you've heard the words 'Yes, you can,' about 5,000 times. That's thirty no's for every yes. This makes for a powerful belief of 'I can't.' --John Assaraf

633. We believe one of the biggest problems against people becoming successful and reaching their goals is their own lack of belief, due to old habits and negative conditioning on the mind winning over.

634. To *conceive*... first you must believe. We visualise and talk about our goals and dreams every single day. By doing this it keeps us focused, real, accountable, determined and action orientated.

635. Expect success... don't just wish and hope for it. You know the old saying… you get what you expect!

636. Did you know that most people are more fearful of being successful than they are at failing? Don't fear success... the rewards are worth it and not only that, who else could you help and inspire along the way?

637. We too have days that we don't feel like working at our success and when this happens, we again ask ourselves… 'Will this wasted day take us closer to our outcome or can we at least take some action to keep up the momentum?'

638. Sometimes we procrastinate because we are afraid of what others will think of us. At the end of the day, it's only the face looking back at you in the mirror that matters most.

639. It's natural for those close to us to attempt to hold us back unknowingly. No one wants to feel left behind, so they'll often (without malice) say and do anything to keep you close to them.

640. Take the hand of a natural leader and follow their footsteps, but only if they have achieved all that you'd like to. Most of the time, there's nothing you'll experience that they have not already.

641. Remember… nothing is more expensive than a lost opportunity.

642. Don't lose sight of your outcome and never ever give up... you owe it to yourself to give it your all. This life isn't a dress rehearsal; it's the real thing so go for it.

643. People often say to us… if you're so good at making money on the Internet why share your secrets with the rest of the world? And the truth is, it's our mission and vision in life to give as many everyday people the opportunity to experience life on their own terms, using eBay and the Internet as their'wealth vehicle.'

644. Once you know *how* to make money on the Internet and become financially free, it becomes natural to want to help others do the same. Whose life could you be making a difference in?

645. We see making money a self-fulfilling act (in a good way of course ;-), however, teaching *others* how to make money by showing them everything you know becomes a selfless act and therefore gives us emotional fulfilment.

646. I (Amanda) failed every subject at school except religion and art and was told I was dumb and would never amount to much. We understand what it takes to stay focused on our dreams and goals and never give up, no matter the odds stacked against us. We believe in you; however, you have to too.

647. Matt was a carpenter with a dream. A dream to get off the tools and create a business that provided a lifestyle that dreams are made of. Do you think that if a carpenter and a failed high school dropout can make it happen, then you can too? Absolutely!

648. When you feel the odds stacked against you, take comfort in the fact that there's always someone else out there who is much worse off than you and somehow gone on to be massively successful.

649. If someone wants your dream more than you do, then there's little chance you'll have true success. Make sure you have good people around you who have your best interests at heart both personally and professionally whom you can confide in.

650. Adversity happens to the best of us. The real winners are those who can get up, brush off and keep on going when things seem almost impossible. So don't let the setbacks you have be the reason to give up. Make them your reason to move forward.

651. There was many a day on this journey when we wanted to throw in the towel, but somehow we just kept going because we were so broke and unhappy with where our lives were at. In your mind, you need to believe that success is your only option and treat that mindset with the dedication and respect it deserves and needs.

652. Even when they laughed at us, we kept our *heads down, and our bums up* and never took our eye off the end result: financial freedom. We had our success blinkers on and refused to take our eyes off the prize.

653. As you grow and head down the success path, your closest friends and family will unconsciously be threatened by what you're doing and where you're going. Accept their comments without judgement, as they don't really understand what you might be going through or how deep the drive in you might be.

654. The more value you give others... the more money you will make. This theory can apply to your relationships too.

655. You'll be paid in exact proportion to the value you give others… never lose sight of this. Make sure you give your eBay customers massive value when they shop with you by offering bonuses.

656. Are you offering a fair exchange of value to the people who you do business with you? Or are you trying to win without letting other people benefit too?

Our Sales Are Now Up To $16,500 Monthly And It Keeps Increasing!

Hi Matt & Amanda and the Bidding Buzz Team,

Shane and I bought the Deluxe EBay Magic Course back in December, 2009. We got off to a slow start but attended your 'Zero To A Million And Beyond' Workshop in March 2010 and it has been all systems go since then. I have found numerous Hot Products from local suppliers and have just completed a few imports from China and they have been easy and very successful imports. Our eBay business is going very strong and continuously growing. Our sales are now up to $16,500 monthly and it keeps increasing and increasing!

In November last year we procrastinated about buying the Ebay Magic Course for days. Finally we decided to buy it because I desperately wanted a change of lifestyle. It has been the best decision of my life. I am now able to work from home and choose the hours I would like to work. We can go on more holidays and we can have weekends off together.

From the bottom of my heart thankyou so much Matt and Amanda for the opportunity you have given us to live the lifestyle we have always wanted. Thanks so much Rachelle for always being there with any questions we may have. I can't thank you enough you have been amazing. We wouldn't have progressed this far without all your help.

We look forward to more success!

Thank you so much,

Amy and Shane

Chapter 9

19 Traits Of A Successful Person

Chapter 9: 19 Traits Of A Successful Person

657. **Big Picture Thinkers.** Successful people have open minds and think big, which in turn attracts circumstances and people to their lives that often help them along their journey.

658. **Self-Belief**. Unless you believe in yourself and your mission don't expect others to. People are always attracted to those who believe in themselves and have the right intent.

659. **Persistence**. To be successful, it's an absolute must that you are persistent. Remember… every'no'is one step closer to a yes!

660. **Confidence.** Act confident and self-assured, even if at times you're not! You will experience confidence if you truly believe in yourself and what you want to achieve.

661. **Can Do Attitude**. You'll become more successful quicker and easier if you're prepared to do just about anything and everything to make it happen. Keep in mind… your intent must be right.

662. **Action Taker**. Like we said before… unless there is constant and never-ending action, you won't enjoy the fruits of success. Take action every chance you get.

663. **Optimism.** Rarely does a pessimistic, negative person enjoy success on any level. If you want all the joys life has to offer, then you must be optimistic and open to accepting abundance into your life.

664. **Take Responsibility**. It's a fact… your past decisions have gotten you to where you are today. If you are not happy with your current circumstances, then take responsibility, make some changes and move forward in a positive manner.

665. **Honesty.** When you have an honest business and you're an honest person who truly wants to give others massive value, you're well and truly on the right path to success on all levels.

666. **Positive Language**. As we said before, use positive language when speaking to others and, most importantly, use it when you speak to your inner self! Your personal language and thoughts will determine your financial destiny.

667. **Reliability.** There's nothing worse than an unreliable person, so if you want success in your life, be reliable! People will come to depend on you and trust you if you are.

668. **Be True To Yourself.** If you can't be true and honest with yourself, then why would someone else trust you? Don't make the mistake of living a life of mediocrity because you don't have the courage to say no when others try to take you off track.

669. **Set High Standards.** If you want a *lifestyle* to die for, whatever that looks like to you, then you must get used to setting high standards. Become a leader, expect nothing but the best and deliver as much to your customers.

670. **High Energy.** We believe that if you're on the right path to success, then high energy comes naturally. Having said this, we're also great believers in maintaining great health through good eating and exercise, which in turn gives you so much energy you'll be blasting a trail to success.

671. **Self-Motivation.** We used to be in the business of *motivating* people with the personal training business, which is a hard game. We believe that if you need to be motivated to getting your dreams and goals, you're likely to fail. Most of the time, truly successful people are naturally self-motivated and tend to inspire others to join them on their journey.

672. **Get Excited.** Do you wake up excited each and every morning? If the answer is no then you're not on the right path. When you are, you wake up excited every day chomping at the bit to get the show on the road! Wow, what a great feeling that is.

673. **Get Educated.** We don't know a single successful person who doesn't invest in continual personal growth and education. The day you think you know it all is the day you start losing it all. Remember this…your just like a tree, either growing or dying.

674. **Get Around Smarter People Than You!** All successful people have mentors to some degree. Our favourite thing is to learn from those who make what we've achieved look pathetic. We love nothing more than stretching our minds to places we've not imagined before and daring ourselves

to make things happen beyond our wildest dreams or understanding. What about you? Who challenges you and your mindset on a daily basis to help you grow beyond your wildest dreams?

675. **Be Money Conscious.** Only those who become 'money conscious' ever accumulate great riches. Money consciousness means that the mind has become so thoroughly saturated with the DESIRE for money that one can see one's self already in possession of it. -*Napoleon Hill*

676. If you don't see great riches in your imagination, you'll never see them in your bank balance.

677. Those who are afraid of new ideas are doomed from the start.

678. Success requires no apologies; failure permits no alibis.

679. If the thing you wish to do is right, and you believe in it, go ahead and do it! Put your dream across, and never mind what 'others' say about you, especially if you meet with temporary defeat or setbacks.

680. One of our favourite sayings is…
"The higher the hurdle…the easier it is to get under it!"
This means you need to look at things from a different perspective and believe that there is almost always another way to tackle a problem.

681. Remember, no more effort is required to aim high in life, to demand abundance and prosperity, than is required to accept misery and even poverty.

I Am Now A Power Seller On Ebay!... I Get To Work Around My 3 Children

Deep down I knew that I could start my own business, unfortunately looking at the various "business" opportunities out there I needed to have a whole heap of cash – something I didn't have!

I stumbled across the Bidding Buzz website and watched the video's of other people who have built their own successful Ebay business following the Bidding Buzz course step by step – I realised that this was totally do-able and on top of that, it was an affordable investment!

I immediately saw the opportunity so I contacted Bidding Buzz and organised for my pack to be sent out to me.

It is definitely not a get rich quick scheme which is comforting because just like any other traditional business it requires a lot of hard work, focus and determination – however – the difference with learning through Bidding Buzz was that I was NEVER on my own as they provided mentoring which means that they 'hold your hand' every step of the way! What a relief that was because I didn't even know the first thing about Ebay let alone starting my own business!

I attended the 3 day workshop which cemented in my mind and heart that what I have invested in by purchasing Ebay Magic Deluxe was not only a"business"but the feeling of empowerment and belief in myself that yeah, I can do this! I not only now own my own business, but I am building a legacy for my children and that all my goals and dreams are closer to becoming a reality!

I am now a Power Seller on Ebay!…I get to work around my 3 children, choose my own hours and don't have to answer to anyone anymore – probably just my husband every now and then…lol..

Thank you Matt, Amanda and your team for providing the tools for me to step out and be all that I can be and more!

Regards
Salome Borg

"Successful people have 3 things in common they all take Ownership, Accountability and Responsibility for their life's circumstances."

Darren J Stephens
International Bestselling Author & Speaker

Chapter 10

Using Advanced Selling Strategies To Explode Your Profits & Save Time

Chapter 10: Using Advanced Selling Strategies...

682. Whether you have a business on eBay or any business for that matter, you simply must act and be professional on every level, if you want suppliers and customers to take you and your business seriously. These handy tips will guide you nicely.

683. Get as many 'eBay icons' as you can... buyers love seeing these icons next to your User ID because it makes you look like a big player!

684. Create an 'About Me' page and the About Me icon will be displayed next to your User ID. Around 17% of shoppers will look at your 'About Me' page before they decide whether or not to shop with you.

685. Your 'About Me' page is all about building *trust* and *credibility* with the potential bidder and explains what you and your business stand for.

686. People buy from those they know like and trust and eBay is no different. Your 'About Me' page is a great opportunity for people to get to know you better as a seller.

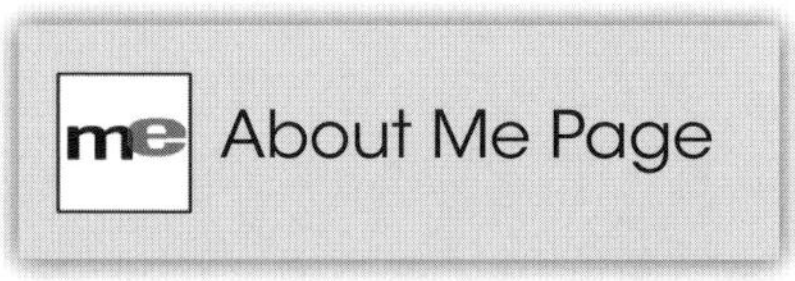

687. Here's where you get to add pictures of yourself and your products if you wish and allow your personality to shine through.

688. You can talk about your products on your 'About Me' page, but don't ramble on about your personal life... keep it to business.

689. Talk about the benefits of why people should shop with you and how great your customer service is.

690. Share your business experience and history to boost your credibility.

691. Don't forget to include links back to your eBay store so buyers can easily get back to your listings and bid on your items!

692. Also include the simple feedback option when setting up your 'About Me' page so potential buyers can see how other buyers rate your service.

693. Include the same banners and logos as you have for your store and listings to keep your branding consistent and not confusing for the buyer.

694. Having a store is also a must if you intend on optimising your profits and maximising all selling opportunities, and there are many reasons why you'd be mad not to have a store.

695. Once you open a store, you'll have the 'red door' icon next to your User ID, which indicates to buyers you have a store.

696. When opening a store you can select from a 'Basic, Featured or Anchored' store level subscription, and the most suitable level will depend on your turnover and how advanced you are on eBay.

697. Generally a 'Basic' store is all you'll need when you're launching your business and a store allows you to have longer durations for your listings.

698. Rather than the usual 1, 3, 5, 7 or 10 days that are available, once you open a store subscription your fixed price listings can also be 30 days or 'Good Til Cancelled'.

699. When listing fixed price items, select the '30 days or Good Til Cancelled' duration and your insertion fees will be reduced significantly for those listings. How great is that!

700. An eBay store is also your own piece of real estate where you customise the colour and layout, so if you don't have one already... go on and open one today!

701. Once you understand the basics of selling on eBay, you can also invest in third party programs, such as **www.auctiva.com**, to create your listings and have many more features at your fingertips.

702. You can save money by listing through Auctiva, after you pay the small monthly subscription fee.

703. The best part of Auctiva is that they host your photos at a cheaper rate than eBay and, because a picture is worth a thousand words, the more you have in your listing the better to show every angle.

704. Auctiva allows you to have up to 24 photos for free in every single listing, whereas eBay will charge you for each additional photo after the first one.

705. Auctiva also offers free scheduling so you can list your items anytime without having to be online, and again eBay charges for this service.

706. Auctiva also offer free listing templates that make your listings really stand out and appear much more professional.

707. You can even create your own Custom Templates or edit their samples. Auctiva allows you to create your listings in HTML or the standard view depending on your computer skills.

708. There is nothing more valuable than time, wouldn't you agree? eBay is the only business we've ever experienced where it's possible to automate up to 90% of the daily tasks (depending on the type of business you have). Here's where the true value of an eBay business is recognised.

709. eBay offer two programs called 'Selling Manager' and 'Selling Manager Pro' that help you automate your business. This can free you up to spend more time with your family and do the things you love.

710. You can automate your feedback, so that you don't ever have to manually leave feedback again!

711. You can also automate the day-to-day emails with buyers when an item is sold, when an item is paid for and even send payment reminders.

712. Many sellers get carried away listing items *(which isn't a bad problem to have ;)*, and don't understand what they're truly making in profits after fees and costs. Keep an eye on your costs to make sure you really are profitable.

713. Using 'Selling Manager Pro' can help you keep an eye on costs, once you know how to fill out the necessary information, which is very basic. You can print or download a monthly report that gives you a complete breakdown of gross sales, eBay fees, PayPal fees, costs, gross profits and *much, much more!*

See the Reporting example below…

Search

:eport

Sale Price	Postage Charged	Gross Sales	Cost of Item	Postage Cost	eBay Fees	PayPal Fees	Total Cost	Total Gain	Sales Tax
AU $1,968.85	AU $540.10	**AU $2,518.35**	AU $753.00	AU $471.00	AU $233.08	AU $68.27	**AU $1,525.35**	**AU $993.00**	AU $0.00

tom oel	Qty	Sale Price	PostageCharged	Gross Sales	Cost ofItem	Postage Cost	eBay Fees	PayPal Fees	Cost	Gain
	1	AU $12.95	AU $5.20	**AU $18.15**	AU $5.00	AU $4.35	AU $1.02	--	**AU $10.37**	**AU $7.78**
	1	AU $49.95	AU $10.60	**AU $60.55**	AU $26.60	AU $9.90	AU $3.95	AU $1.75	**AU $42.20**	**AU $18.35**

714. Did you know... you can actually 'automate' your eBay business by up to 90%? That's all the little mundane bits and pieces you need to do on a daily basis. Of course this depends on how you run your business and what type of eBay business you choose to own. However, this is what we have been able to do and now teach others to do with our eBay Magic home study program. You see, automating a business can and will truly set you free. After all, isn't *freedom* the game behind the game?

"Unless you're willing to fail, and have another go, success won't happen."

Darren J Stephens
International Bestselling Author & Speaker

Chapter 11

More Ways To Increase Productivity And Profits

Chapter 11: More Ways To Increase Productivity...

715. When we started our eBay business, we began with the end in mind and thought about how we could turn the business into an asset that would become very valuable. Here's the thing… if you can automate your eBay business while still bringing in great profits, can you imagine how much demand you'd get if you put it up for sale? You see, freedom is what we all want and eBay is the perfect freedom business, if that's what you're chasing, as we were!

716. The easiest eBay businesses to automate are ones where you sell clusters of products within a category. In other words, you don't want to become a junkyard on eBay as it's hard to automate. The idea is to become the expert in your chosen category and dominate it to the best of your ability.

717. Start off slow and steady, building it up one product at a time so you get it right. By doing this, you can more easily automate it and then move on to other categories. In the beginning, you may want to go berserk and be everything to everyone; however, you'll be glad if you follow the steps and create something worthwhile.

718. A large number of people who sell on eBay do it simply as a hobby to bring in extra cash; however, if you really understand what you're doing and have the right information, you can create a valuable asset while becoming cash and time rich.

719. Right from the start, take your eBay business seriously or it will always give you a part-time 'hobby' income.

720. Plan to set up the right way from the beginning and get the advice of an accountant for company structures, etc., so you can plan your possible exit strategy. We know of people who have sold eBay businesses for millions!

721. What if you set up one eBay business, automated it as much as possible and continued the pattern? Do you think you may have valuable assets you could sell later?

722. In our opinion, there's absolutely no point in going into business unless you have a clear outcome and plan that will give you and your family what you want.

723. If you want a full time income from your eBay business, understand you'll have to put in extra effort at the start and make sacrifices.

724. There's nothing wrong with wanting a *part-time* income from eBay. Remember… follow your dreams and don't worry about what others think.

725. The beauty about eBay is that if you love what you're currently doing for a living and don't want to give it up, you don't have to! Your eBay business can be tailored to suit you and your family.

726. Unless you're making a profit, there's no point in having a business! That's why you must have an exact plan of when profits are likely to occur. Here are a few pointers to take into consideration.

727. The difference between incomings and outgoings is your profit. Unless you know exactly what's going on in your business it will be impossible to know if you are making money.

728. Too many eBay sellers believe they are making a lot of money when in fact they haven't even taken their costs of goods sold or any other outgoings into consideration. Do you know what your running costs are?

729. In the early stages of your business try not to over capitalise and keep your overheads lean.

730. You're in business to make a profit, so make sure you run your business cost-effectively and enjoy your rewards.

731. Keeping your overheads low is easy if you think through what you really need in your eBay business. Keep the emotion out of business… there's no place for it.

732. Don't go renting big, expensive warehouses if you can get away with using a cheaper storage shed or even your own garage or spare room!

733. Just because you run your eBay business from home, doesn't mean you have to act cheap. Treat your business just as you would if you had an expensive shop front!

734. Keep in mind that in Australia, the actual eBay fees are really paid to eBay Switzerland. This means their fees do not include GST and can't be included as tax credits when doing your GST BAS.

735. Shop online to find shipping paraphernalia, which can be much cheaper than buying it retail.

736. Choose a smart Internet plan that allows you to upload your photos and listing more affordably.

737. Take advantage and use 'Skype' *(it's free ;-)* whenever you can or invest in an international calling card if you need to call overseas suppliers. Remember…you're in business and every dollar in your account adds up!

738. Buy postage satchels and envelopes in bulk quantities for better pricing, and when wrapping items, choose the right packaging to optimize postage costs. You'd be surprised at how high the cost will jump if you use the wrong packaging.

739. Shop around for courier and postage prices… they vary greatly. Don't forget to use your negotiation skills!

740. If you happen to also be an eBay shopper, why not re-use some of the packaging and boxes to save money and look after our environment?

741. Use the automation tools available through eBay to give better customer service and reduce your staffing needs as things can get out of hand easily if you don't stay on top of it all.

742. When your business grows to a certain level, you can have couriers and Australia post come to you. This saves time and money so you can get on with the important stuff.

743. Source your products as cheaply as possible to save money. If you can, buy larger quantities of stock to save even more money.

744. Run your eBay business from home for as long as you can before venturing out into the commercial world where costs can rise dramatically.

745. Offer postage discounts if customers buy multiple products from you to encourage multiple sales. Buyers love to save as much as possible on shipping costs so bundle packages when you can.

746. Once you nail all the ways to maximise your profits with your eBay business, it's time to engage in advanced strategies that will surely take your business to a whole new level you may not have thought possible. Here're a few tips to get you thinking!

747. Most serious sellers on eBay aspire to become a 'PowerSeller' and are among the most successful sellers on eBay in terms of product sales and customer satisfaction.

748. Among eBay sellers, a designation of PowerSeller status is given to approximately only 4%, which gives you an idea of how many sellers really know what they're doing!

749. Becoming a PowerSeller is a question of following eBay's guidelines, especially if you want to keep it, so you should be up to date on eBay's policies and guidelines.

750. PowerSellers can get great advantages on eBay, access to special areas and, on some platforms, even discounts on eBay fees!

751. There are four PowerSeller levels you can achieve (on eBay.com), including Silver, Gold, Platinum and Titanium depending on your gross sale amount.

752. To qualify for the 'PowerSeller program' in Australia, you need to make average monthly sales of $3,000 for Silver, $10,000 for Gold, $25,000 for Platinum and $150,000 for Titanium per month for three consecutive months – so aim high!

753. You must also ensure that you have an overall feedback rating of 100, which is at least 98% positive, and provide outstanding customer service.

754. Things like low DSR's *(Detailed Seller Ratings)*, unpaid accounts and customer complaints can mean you'll risk losing the valuable PowerSeller icon.

755. As a PowerSeller always stay up to date with trends and changes in eBay. Scan the 'Community' board for PowerSeller and eBay updates.

756. Plan to be organised. PowerSellers deal with such a large volume of business that they need to develop systems to run their business smoothly and routinely.

757. As a PowerSeller, you also have the opportunity to qualify for "Top-Rated" seller status, which is currently available in the US and UK.

758. 'Top-Rated' sellers are also PowerSellers who have achieved the highest levels of customer satisfaction, and they receive additional benefits. Top Rated Seller is the new version of PowerSeller being used in the UK and America. At the time of writing this book, it had not been implemented into the Australian eBay market place.

759. All levels of PowerSellers are eligible for Top-Rated seller status and your search standing is increased as a Top-Rated seller. This of course increases your chances of more sales and higher profits, so it's well worth going for!

760. You can enjoy discounts of up to 20% off your Final Value Fees as a Top-Rated seller, which means even more money in your pocket!

The road of 'average' is paved by good intentions;
The road of 'greatness' is paved with accomplishments…

W.Clement Stone

"If you're passionate, Persistent and have a Powerful mindset you can achieve anything."

Darren J Stephens
International Bestselling Author & Speaker

Chapter 12

Hot Tips, Strategies & Proven Ways To Make More Money And Still Keep Things Simple

761. eBay is a search engine, and when buyers are looking for certain items, eBay sorts the results into what they class as a 'Best Match' in the search results. The aim is to reward top sellers who give great service a better search result ranking. Ultimately, with eBay, it's all about giving the buyer the best experience so they'll keep coming back to the website.

762. There are many components that eBay considers when sorting the results out on the display page for buyers, and you need to ensure you're at the top of the search page to get traffic to your listings. One of the components is your 'DSRs' (Detailed Seller Ratings) and they are an extremely important part of your eBay business.

763. When buyers leave you positive feedback, they can also rate you on certain aspects of the sale, including how accurate the item description was, how satisfied they were with the communication, how quickly did you ship the item, and how reasonable you were with the shipping and handling charges. As you can see, you really need to be on top of your game if you want to get your listings high in the search results.

764. Put on your buyers hat and put yourself in their shoes. Begin thinking like a buyer instead of a seller and brainstorm ideas of things that *YOU* would want to experience and that would make you happy as a buyer. Be a hero to your customers and remember you want them to remember you in a positive way... give them 5 star service and in return you can expect 5 star feedback ratings!

Detailed Seller Ratings (last 12 months)

Criteria	Average rating	Number of ratings
Item as described	★★★★★	12298
Communication	★★★★★	12281
Shipping time	★★★★★	12272
Shipping and handling charges	★★★★★	12229

765. Implementing systems from the start will help you keep tabs on all costs for your business, so you can see how profitable it is at any given moment. You can do this online or the old-fashioned 'pen and paper' method.

766. Because there is a lot less overhead working from home with an eBay business, it gives you more capital to spend on stock, which is of course where the profits are hiding ;-)

767. An eBay business can cost anywhere from $150 a month to run to a full scale $500 a month, depending on how streamlined you run your business, which is still small pennies compared to a retail business.

768. Choosing cost-effective shipping companies or methods can put money back in your pocket, and often couriers can negotiate their rates, once they know you're a long-term reliable business.

769. The packaging of your items can also add to your overall shipping costs, so make sure you're looking at all alternatives and not settling for the first option.

770. Just like in traditional brick & mortar businesses, you'll need to keep a close eye on all eBay fees and charges because they will have a major effect on your overall profit margin.

771. Keep a record of your costs and profits for tax purposes. You can sign up for Selling Manager Pro on eBay, which can help you record all the money going into your business and what is your net eBay profit at the end of the month. This won't include your other business costs; it primarily calculates the activity happening within eBay.

772. Don't forget PayPal costs need to be integrated into your cost of running an eBay business too. Fees each month can add up to be a large amount if most of your transactions are done through there.

773. There are so many benefits of running a home based business, make sure you talk to your accountant about deductions you can make as an added benefit.

774. Each eBay business will be very individual and the costs associated with different types of businesses can vary according to the type of listings you have or the prices you're starting your items at. Also, it comes down to whether it's a part-time hobby or full time business and of course how many educational tools you are using to grow and streamline your eBay business.

775. If you're new to eBay, don't automatically go for all the shiny bells, whistles and upgrades, as this will shock you at the end of the month when you get invoiced from eBay!

776. When eBay business owners go on holidays, their business can close without ongoing overheads to continue payment on. Alternatively, for short absences, their business can continue to operate without them if they have the processes in place we've talked about throughout this book.

777. If you do intend to take breaks from your business for whatever reason, make sure you plan these things in advance and hopefully you won't have any hidden surprises later on.

778. Keep your eyes peeled for opportunity every chance you get, even when you go on holidays and trips. People from all walks of life seem to love talking about eBay, so bring the subject up whenever you can!

779. While on vacation, why not call into or ring different companies who have stock you may be interested in selling? You just never know your luck and you can then look at making part of your trip a tax deduction.

780. Write a list of all your friends and family and different businesses they work in or know. Who out there could put you in touch with suppliers for your eBay business?

781. When talking to suppliers, you must sell them on why 'you're' the right person to sell their goods. Give them a good picture of what they can expect if they do business with you.

782. There are many ways to list and sell items on eBay. Why not try them all to find the best recipe for success? You never know which strategy might work best unless you try them all.

783. A 'Reserve' price is the amount the bidding must reach before you will sell your item; however, this option isn't available in every category or eBay website, so do your homework.

784. If you have a unique or high demand product, it's probably best to sell via Auction format to maximize your profits.

785. If you don't know the real value of an item, but believe it has a high value, your best bet is to auction it and see how it goes! *(That is of course if you're not too attached to the outcome ;-)*

786. For mainstream retail items, a Buy It Now price can be a quick and easy way of selling your products on eBay.

787. Every serious eBay seller needs a store. In fact, it's getting harder and harder to make money unless you know what you're doing, so make sure you learn the rules of the game.

788. Having an eBay store allows your buyers to browse everything you have for sale and is a great way to get multiple sales from one buyer.

789. Everything you put up for auction on eBay shows up in your eBay store. Here's where you can get lucky and make more sales than you bargained for!

790. If you have items that are slow moving, pop them in your eBay store. Eventually they'll probably sell. Don't forget to try bundling things together for slow moving items, as this may bring interest where there weren't any previously.

791. Conversion rates fluctuate depending on product demand and pricing, so prepare for these possibilities in your budget.

792. Always be prepared to let go of your 'drop shipper' if you feel trouble brewing, like stock continually running out and poor feedback from your customers.

793. In the early stages of starting your eBay business, don't try to grow too fast until you really know what you're doing. The bad feedback isn't worth it, so make sure you have a mentor or follow the footsteps of successful sellers only ;-)

794. Steady and controlled growth really is a major key to success as an eBay seller. We've seen a few sellers come and go simply because they couldn't manage their growth and stock levels.

795. Having an eBay business gives you a competitive advantage over a brick and mortar business because you can predict sales and competition far more accurately.

796. The other advantage of selling online compared to a shopfront is that if your products are not moving and the market changes, you can quickly adapt.

797. If you pay too much for your stock upfront, it's going to be hard to make a decent profit selling on eBay. You make your money when you buy your stock at a fair price. If this happens to you, consider going back to traditional places like flea markets or garage sales.

798. Buying stock to sell on eBay is a little like buying real estate. You make your money *going in*.

799. If you want to sell clothing on eBay, make sure you use a mannequin or a real person to model them. Your buyers will get a much better feel for what they'll get.

800. Use traffic counters to see how many visitors you get to your auctions. This will come in handy if you're testing different variations of your listings.

801. Don't make the shipping process a nightmare for buyers… if it all seems too hard, they'll move on to another seller who makes it easy.

802. Make sure you've worked out your fees before you start selling. You'd be surprised how quickly they can add up later!

803. eBay has really cracked down on sellers who overcharge shipping rates. Keep them fair and reasonable to avoid low DSRs and negative feedback.

804. Keep an eye on what your competition charges for shipping… don't let yours creep up too much higher or you'll lose sales.

805. When you ship parcels out, give them a good shake in a few different directions to see how secure your packaging is. You should be able to drop it onto the ground without breaking anything, because there's no doubt it's going to get knocked around on the way to your customer!

806. The stronger the packaging, the better your chances are of parcels turning up to your customers undamaged. Use good quality packaging materials; it will be worth it in the long run.

807. Another tip when sending out parcels is to not use newspaper, as the black print will rub off onto the items and spoil them. Use white butcher paper, bubble wrap, packing foam or plain tissue paper, etc.

808. Using 'Pay Per Click' advertising is another advanced strategy some buyers use to drive traffic to their eBay auctions and store. Don't forget that each click costs money so keep a close eye on this.

809. Another advanced strategy is to build your own website to promote your products outside of eBay.

810. If you do have a website outside of eBay to promote your products, it's vital to have good content and relevant keywords to help the optimization of the website.

811. If you decide to add links from other websites, it's very important that the information is relevant to what you're selling, otherwise the search engines receive mixed messages and won't rank your website high in the search results.

812. To drive more traffic to your eBay store, you can write reviews and guides relating to your product niche, as they actually get ranked in the search engines as well. This means your guides can be found in Google and Yahoo, etc., giving you access to a global search market.

813. If you have many guides that are voted on by the general public, you can get an extra icon next to your eBay user ID, giving you more credibility in the buyers mind.

814. Why not start a blog to attract new customers to your eBay business? A blog is really easy to set up, and there are plenty of free resources to help you. Just go to Google and you'll see for yourself!

815. Include things in your blog such as relevant news and updates about your products, coming products, specials, and special occasions… It's about having a conversation with your readers and keeping it interesting.

816. If you have a website outside of your eBay business, one of the first things you must concentrate on is building a database of customers.

817. Don't email your list with non-relevant information… it's the fastest way to lose them!

818. Make sure you email your list with good content and don't try to sell them something each time. We only ever provide offers to our database a few times a year… the rest of the time we educate them, which they love.

819. Most people think their lists of customers are simply there to sell to. This could not be further from the truth… they're there because they look to you as the expert and to give them content they're interested in. Only after you have fully won their trust and respect will they buy from you.

820. Building a solid database with people who know, like and trust you becomes extremely valuable, so don't ever send them rubbish emails trying to sell them non-relevant stuff! They'll unsubscribe in a heartbeat!

821. Make sure you have an unsubscribe link on the bottom of all your email correspondence. There's nothing worse than getting nuisance emails if you're not interested! And anyway, you only want people on your list who are interested in what you have to say, right?

822. Make sure your content is always cutting edge and up to date, so you get seen as the leader in your field of expertise. We are forever doing courses and upgrading our knowledge, and see mentoring and coaching as an "investment" in our future, rather than a "cost."

Chapter 13

Accelerate Your Growth By Finding A Mentor Who Has Blazed The Trail Before You & Succeeded

Chapter 13: Accelerate Your Growth...

823. It's without a doubt that successful people from all walks of life have mentors in their lives to help them get there faster and avoid nasty pitfalls along the way.

824. The biggest tip I can share here is this… Never accept advice from someone who does not have the result you want…. they're not qualified to give it to you! Here are a few reasons why you'd consider having mentors in business.

825. Mentors have usually blazed a trail and can remove some of the risk for you. They have already spent their time and money working the various systems out so you don't have to.

826. A worthwhile mentor is one that tells you as it is… the good, the bad and the ugly points of your business.

827. You can learn how to deliver better customer service based on their previous experience. Learn from their mistakes, not yours!

828. Improve your productivity by asking them how they do tasks more quickly and easily.

829. Save money using their tips on cost saving strategies and eliminate making the same mistakes people have made before you.

830. Fast track your processes based on their skills and knowledge, and use their network of associates and colleagues to meet like-minded people.

831. Join mentoring groups as well to get access to more people who could help promote your business.

832. Ask mentors for tips on gaining interest from the "Press" both locally and nationally.

833. Great places to meet mentors are the Chamber of Commerce, Breakfast Groups, Schools, Universities, Seminars, and Word Of Mouth.

834. Interview specialists to get to know them and possibly build a relationship over time for mentoring.

835. Only ask advice from mentors if you are prepared to listen and take action on their advice. There is nothing a mentor dislikes more than a student who wastes their time by not implementing the help given.

836. The biggest compliment you can give a mentor is to state your goals and then follow through on what you said you would. Mentors love seeing other people achieve too.

837. When courting a mentor and receiving ongoing mentoring, make sure you pay their costs when possible. This could include paying for lunch, coffee, travel, etc. Mentors love being appreciated and the little things count.

838. Be prepared to feel uncomfortable when stretching yourself to learn and grow. If you're not uncomfortable, then you're not growing.

839. Make sure to take full responsibility for your own actions and outcomes with your business. Never blame your mentor if you try things and they don't work. Mentors only give advice based on best practice but not every strategy would apply to you and your business. This is where you simply must "test and measure" until you have reached your desired outcome.

840. When it comes to making money on eBay, there are a lot of things to do that don't necessarily bring in profits. Make sure you spend most of your time on activities that produce income and allocate unproductive time accordingly.

841. Working from home sometimes can be a downfall if you're not time-managed. Make a point of writing down what activity your doing every fifteen minutes or so and see how much of this is income producing.

842. Make sure your friends and family know that when you work from home you still need to get your work done. Often they'll think you're not working simply because you are at home. This couldn't be further from the truth.

843. The more you put into your business, the more you get out of it (in theory anyway). If you're spending too much time chasing products you can't get your hands on, then move on. Don't let your emotions get in the way.

844. The more you can systemise your eBay business and automate it, the more time you can spend on ways to bring in more money.

845. Each night before you finish up, write your "to do" list for the next day. Start with the hardest tasks first and move down to the easiest as the day progresses.

846. Isolate all your daily tasks and then write up all steps associated with each. Systemise each step as much as possible and allocate them in number of importance.

847. Don't waste precious time on tasks that don't bring money in. Spend the largest portion of your day bringing money in... the rest will wait.

848. If you work from home, make sure you start the day with your agenda on hand. Treat your business like a business and you will make more money than if you treat it like a hobby.

849. Only take breaks during the day if it's necessary. The more you do, the more you make!

850. In the early stages of your business, try to work normal business hours. As you grow and automate daily tasks, only then should you relax a little.

851. Once you've started to automate daily tasks, you can either take time off or consider going into other eBay markets to make even more streams of income!

852. Research is constant and never ending, so enjoy the process.

853. Keep your "eBay goggles" on every time you leave the house... you never know what opportunity awaits you around the corner.

854. As you grow your business, make sure you plan to work "on"your business and not so much"in"your business.

855. Make sure you spend time every day working on your mindset. This is the most important part of the day in our opinion.

856. Procrastination steals your dreams away. Avoid it at all costs.

857. Take some time to exercise every day, even if it's a walk around the block. Fresh air and exercise clears your mind and helps you come up with great ideas when you least expect it!

858. In the early days of starting our eBay business, it was normal to put in 12-hour days. After 6 months or so, it was automated to the point it took only about 10 hours a week to run. Were the long days in the beginning worth it? You bet!

859. In business, you have great days and crappy days, so get used to it. When you're having a crappy day, just remember all the reasons why you got into business in the first place. You will smile again ;-)

860. Be aware of dream stealers... they'll interfere with your productivity and slow you down from realizing your dreams.

861. Sometimes it's best to keep things close to your chest while trying to gain"momentum"in the early stages of your business.

862. One of the biggest reasons people fail in business is the lack of momentum. Avoid the next "shiny object" at all costs.

863. It's easy to get momentum in your business if you're organized and know your outcome. Have a clear picture of what you want your business to look like, so that it's easier for you to stay focused and on track.

864. There are so many exciting ways of making money on eBay that it's easy to get distracted. Only focus on what's going to give you the lifestyle you've been looking for and nothing else.

865. Even after many years of selling on eBay, I continually look for hungry markets to sell into on eBay. It keeps me up to date and open-minded.

866. It's a good idea to get yourself into a daily routine so you don't go off the rails and lose momentum. Do the same tasks each day so it becomes second nature. Before long, you'll get so fast and so good at it that it'll become a breeze.

867. The earlier you begin your day and get things done, the more time you have to think about how you can increase sales and profits.

868. Spend at least an hour a day researching new product ideas and markets.

869. Make it a habit to talk to suppliers as often as possible. Before long, they'll be coming to you!

870. Have a special "eBay room" if you can, so that you can leave everything set up and ready to go!

871. If you're doing your own shipping, set it up like a conveyor belt to keep things running smoother and faster, and keep your work place neat and tidy. It helps productivity.

872. Don't finish your day until you have ticked everything off your "to do" list. You will feel much better and be able to keep on top of things easier.

873. If you go on a holiday, try not to close your eBay business as it slows momentum and reduces profits. Have a friend or relative ship for you if you can. We've even travelled overseas with eBay products in our suitcase, so we could ship no matter where we were in the world!

874. Never before has there been a better time to start your own home-based family business using eBay as your vehicle. Many of our happy customers have their whole family involved and now enjoy more choices, more time and cash flow.

875. Here's a way for the kids to earn pocket money! Get them to do easy tasks like wrapping packages and writing dockets, etc. eBay… a business the whole family can be involved in!

876. When you're going into business with family or friends, you need to work out "who does what?" Here's some tips on splitting the roles so you don't lose your mind! (Or your partner! ;-)

877. When we first started our eBay business, there were so many things to do, we didn't know who was doing what. Soon enough, we realised that if we wanted to"work together"and"stay together", we needed some clear boundaries in the workplace.

878. Here are a few ideas you may want to take on board.... The first thing we did was determine who was good at what jobs and what jobs did we actually like doing.

879. Next we divided the jobs equally, and called them"pink jobs"and"blue jobs". Amanda took care of all the"pink jobs"and Matt took care of all the"blue jobs."

880. Some pink jobs consisted of customer service, researching new and hot markets, talking to suppliers, printing the dockets out each morning to be ready for shipping and answering customer questions. Some of the blue jobs consisted of the listing process, taking photos, scheduling times we wanted items to finish, internet marketing and all that involved the"techi"things Amanda didn't like much!

881. Our advice is to pick what you like and what you're good at and focus on that! Everything else can be delegated to someone who does a better job! We never focus on things we don't like or we're not great at. It's a waste of our time and can be stressful for no purpose.

882. We also don't believe in wasting time trying to learn things you don't enjoy doing or are not great at. At the end of the day you go into business to have choices and, in our opinion, one of the benefits is surrounding yourself with people who do some things better than you do!

883. Even after many years of selling on eBay, I still spend a lot of time on product and market research, while Matt watches over the"techi"side of things. Working on things you like and do well ensures your working relationship lasts longer!

884. If you're working with your life partner in this business, then we suggest you get your roles sorted out early in the process to avoid unnecessary misunderstandings as the business grows.

885. Another thing we learnt from the start, being in business together is sometimes hard to"switch off"at the end of the day, so what we did to survive was to close the office door at 5pm and walk away.

886. Having said that… I used to sneak her computer into the lounge after 5pm because she became addicted to eBay (and still is ;-) and to watching the money come in every night! I just couldn't help myselfherself!

887. In the early months… I even used to take her laptop to bed with meher to watch auctions finishing. Now, my suggestion is that you don't copy me asher it's not very healthy they tell us! Yeah… good luck with that!

888. A lot of people are nervous about working with their"life partner"; however, we have loved every moment of it and wouldn't change it for the world.

889. The secret to working together and staying together is having respect for each other and taking responsibility for your roles in the business. Once you commit to your roles in the business, you'll have no one to blame when things go south, other than yourself!

890. When we worked full-time in our eBay business, we rarely argued because we knew what we had to do every day. Before long, we were so fast and so good at it, our business only took a couple of hours a day to run and it turned over thousands of dollars a week!

891. Whether you work with your life partner or a business partner in general, all the above rules apply. Great communication is key to having an easy business relationship.

892. You're not a mind reader and neither is your partner, so talk about things all the time to avoid misunderstandings.

893. If you're going into business with a business partner outside your personal relationship, make sure you're both very clear on your desired outcome before you go in.

894. If you both want different things from the one business, it's not worth going in together from the start.

895. You cannot be rigid with your ideas and views when it comes to business… you must evolve and move with the times and the market.

896. Treat your roles in the business very seriously… what's working for you today, may end in disaster tomorrow!

897. Never take your eye off the ball, even when you manage to automate a lot of your daily processes. Things on eBay can change in a heartbeat!

898. Review your business plans often, as eBay changes regularly and so does the market. As you've already read, we only have a one-page business plan because things in this business change so rapidly.

899. Don't be scared of change… it's exciting and keeps you fresh and interested. Most people hate change, so here's where you can get the edge if you're on top of your game!

900. Testing and measuring your results is key when it comes to being successful on eBay, and that means every element of it. Your listings, your headlines, your keywords…in fact the list goes on.

901. Although our staff practically run our eBay business these days, rarely a day goes by when we don't run our eye over the listings to see if it's on track.

902. Sometimes when you're so close to your business, it's easy to miss important things that make you money. Make sure you have a mentor who can help you maximize profits in minimum time.

903. In the early stages of your eBay business, it's easy to become "consumed" with it, as it's so exciting. We don't really have a remedy for that one because we're still consumed by it and can spend up to ten hours a day just looking at hot, untapped markets? What's one to do?

904. If you don't have a partner in this business… don't worry. Just work out all the roles you need to fill, do what you want and pass the rest on when you can afford to do so.

905. One of the things we love most about having an eBay business is that you can do this even if you're by yourself! It's easy once you know what to do and how to do it.

906. Just as we were typing that last tip… we made a $65.00 sale! You see, we each have a little pop up eBay screen on our computer that makes a little noise when we sell something! Now you can see why we have this "eBay addiction" problem going on right?

907. We use Apple's Mac laptops and our preferred browser is Firefox. It still allows us to use all of the eBay features that might not be visible if you use Safari. The eBay feature is a Firefox add-on you can download for free.

908. Never before has there been a better time to start an eBay business, no matter your background, age, or education. If we can sit here sharing our tips and tricks with you while we make money, then so can you! Go for it, you'll love yourself for taking the leap!

"Outer Success is a direct reflection of your inner success."

Darren J Stephens
International Bestselling Author & Speaker

Chapter 14

Hot Tips To Help You Sell More!

Chapter 14: Hot Tips To Help You Sell More!

909. Around 70 – 80% of eBay buyers prefer to pay for items with PayPal, so make sure this is one of your preferred methods.

910. Not everything you list will sell the first time. Make sure you list it at least 3-5 times, changing key factors or testing your keywords each time, or you can try bundling them with other items, which may help sell them faster!

911. Before you buy any stock, know exactly what it will cost you to get it to your doorstep or warehouse, plus try to estimate how much profit you're likely to make.

912. Try to source stock from people who aren't already suppling heaps of other eBay sellers. You'll just get into a price war, which won't work for anyone long term.

913. If you notice certain items are getting lots of attention from buyers, why not see if you can source it too?

914. Did you know that the average selling price of all items on eBay is just $25?

915. Make sure you cross promote your items in your eBay store for more sales. Having an eBay Store often results in customers bidding on more than one of your products.

916. Make sure you spread out your listing finishing times, as this enables buyers to bid for more than one item and attempt to win multiple items from you.

917. Profit margins vary wildly on eBay depending on what products sell and who the sellers are. Try to accept that and manage your own stress levels if this is new to you.

918. The more educated you are about selling on eBay, the more profits you can make.

919. Don't forget to factor your labour time into your running costs.

920. Drop shipping makes you vulnerable to unhappy customers and negative feedback, so it pays to possibly use another eBay ID just for drop shipping.

921. Be patient…success takes time to master!

922. Try to match your eBay user ID to an available Internet Domain name. That way your emails can be associated with your user ID and your eBay customers will recognise communications from you in their email.

923. Be passionate about your eBay business and its success. You get what you expect anyway, so why not shoot for the stars?

924. Find categories and sub-categories to sell in that are not already flooded with other sellers.

925. Always under-promise and over-deliver when it comes to customer service. They'll reward you by shopping again and again with you.

926. The lowest price doesn't always get the bidders. Great value and customer service does though.

927. Many sellers stunt their growth and success due to stubbornness to move into other categories when necessary. Things change, so be prepared to change with the times.

928. Just because you're a successful seller in one category on eBay doesn't mean you'll be successful in others.

929. Make sure you continue to test and measure your results. The eBay market is ever-changing and so must you!

930. Be flexible when moving into new categories… what worked in one category may not work in another!

931. Once you discover a hot market on eBay, find profitable niche markets within it. There are so many, you'd be surprised.

932. Let companies that have surplus stock find you by creating a website that describes what services you offer.

933. Don't forget to test which day of the week is best for finishing auctions. Of course, if the market allows… try to sell something every day of the week!

934. Be aware of how social events, TV and holidays, etc., can affect your business and your profit margins.

935. Make sure you work on your negotiation skills so it becomes second nature when talking to potential suppliers.

936. If you sell, or plan to sell a range of different products in different categories, then you must consider setting up a unique User ID for each range. You don't want to look like a junk yard or catalogue seller.

937. If you like to buy as well as sell on eBay, then you should use a different account. You will look more professional as a seller and of course you keep your buying habits private!

938. Regularly check your competitor's auctions to see what they're up to and what you can learn from them, both good and bad that is! Don't forget that part of your research is to keep an eye on new competitors entering into your market.

939. Why not buy something from your competitors to see how well their business systems are set up, especially the customer service part! You can add your competitors to your "Favourite Sellers" list to monitor their new auctions and to see what they're up to.

940. We've even arbitraged from our competition and bought products we knew we could turn around at the right price. Sometimes they are not as skilled as you and you can sneakily make money from their misfortune.

941. Don't forget to sign up for different newsletters from sellers who sell things you're interested in. It's amazing what you can learn from them. Competitors come and go in the eBay market place so keep your eyes peeled for opportunity.

942. If you want to dominate any category on eBay, you must be able to get an ongoing supply of products to sell in that market. Here's where it's important to have more than one supplier for each of your products.

943. If you set your start price too high, you have way less chance of starting a "bidding war." Let buyers play the bidding game by starting your auctions as low as you can.

944. Don't forget to test ending items during the day depending on your target market; who knows there could be a whole second market at a different finishing time.

945. Shill bidding is when a seller gets friends or family to bid on his/her own items in order to drive up the end price. This practice is highly illegal on eBay and we recommend you don't get into it.

946. Avoid buying from sellers who have a lot of negative feedback. There may be a number of reasons why they do, however avoid them if you can.

947. Announce weekly or monthly discounts, specials and updates to your VIP customers. You will greatly increase the chance of more sales.

948. Encourage buyers to opt in to your newsletter during the checkout process. Here's where you then get the chance to let them know every time you get more relative stock into your business.

949. Why not encourage your customers to add *YOU* to their favourite sellers list. This way they will automatically be updated with what's happening in your business, which could lead to more sales.

950. If your target market is selling to teenagers, understand that you may have more unpaid item problems and unclear communication, simply because of their age and lack of understanding of all eBay rules. Many sellers carve out a very lucrative business on eBay selling thousands of items to "teenagers" everyday of the week.

951. Why not video yourself showing prospective buyers how much care you take when packaging items. People love to know how much you care! Video is a great way for you to describe how to use items you're selling, especially if you find it hard to put into words! Make sure you use lots of pictures too.

952. It's true you know, the more you give, the more you will receive and once you're making decent money on eBay, a great way to give back to the community is through eBay.

953. eBay helps individuals and organizations raise funds for charity and you can list items and give all or part of the proceeds to charity through the "eBay Giving Works" program.

954. You can donate to the charities featured on eBay, including protecting the environment, saving animals, fighting breast cancer or eliminating poverty, just to name a few.

 You can also choose your own charity, as long as it's an organisation or registered as a licensed charity in order to conduct charitable fundraising activities.

955. Once you have registered your charity, you'll receive a charity icon up near your eBay user ID which can drive more business to your store.

956. If you want to donate a percentage of your earnings to a charity, all you have to do is pick your charity and the percentage that you want to donate, and eBay will do the rest for you. Too easy!

957. There are over 2,500 registered charities you can support on eBay and you can donate between 10 - 100% of your sales to help others.

The idea is to fall in love with your customers, not your product or service.
Let your customers grow your business for you.

"Wealth is not a matter of intelligence it's a matter of passion & persistence."

Darren J Stephens
International Bestselling Author & Speaker

Chapter 15

How Does The Economy Really Affect eBay And Tips To Stay Ahead Of The Competition

Chapter 15: How Does The Economy Really...

958. "Economic Ups and Downs" - Whenever you're looking at getting into business, it doesn't matter whether times are good or times are tough, people will always give you a reason not to get in.

959. When the market takes a downturn, people naturally turn to places like eBay to search out bargains, so go for it.

960. People love to shop online because they know if they look hard enough, there's a bargain to be found every moment of every day!

961. There's never been a better time for you to get into selling on eBay and giving bargain hunters the deals they're looking for.

962. When the general public are looking for ways to save money, they tend to stay at home more and shop online as it saves time and money.

963. If you're an importer, be careful and understand that there may be times when the dollar drops dramatically, which affects your profit margins.

964. Getting into business is risky whether the market is up or down. It's how you look at it and how you plan for success in both markets that makes all the difference

965. In the early stages of starting your eBay business, plan to invest a large portion of your profits back into your business in case the market changes unexpectedly.

966. When you have an eBay business, expect good days and bad days as eBay markets change constantly. At the end of the day, we can't control the outside world, so focus on what you can control… your business and how you treat your customers.

967. Depending on the financial markets, your currency could go up or down against the US Dollar, and this can affect the cost of goods and also your profit margins.

968. In tough times you can sell entertainment products such as, board games, card games, chess sets, and computer games, as people tend to stay and entertain at home.

969. Paying Your Taxes… Is it necessary with your eBay Business? Each country or state can be different when it comes to taxes so make sure you get the right advice from your accountant.

970. In Australia, we have two types of taxes: GST (Goods & Services Tax) and then the normal company tax. In Australia, all sale prices on eBay are inclusive of GST if you have income over $75,000 per annum.

971. In the UK they have a similar tax on goods and services and it's called VAT (Value Added Tax).

972. In America, this is generally called a Sales Tax and can vary from state to state.

973. Many people start out as eBay Hobbyists and as they grow, they may need to set up a company, as taxes could be due.

974. An eBay business is no different than a normal business in most countries when it comes to paying taxes on the income. In Australia, there is no GST tax credit for your eBay fees, as you are billed by eBay Switzerland.

975. It's important to keep a record of all international sales as they have different tax implications than local sales. For any further clarification, please consult your local tax expert, as rules could have changed since the time of writing this book.

976. If your eBay business grows to the point of turning over $75,000 annually, then legislation requires that you register for GST.

977. To register for GST in Australia, you'll need to complete an application form, which is available from the ATO. This can be done electronically at **www.business.gov.au**.

978. If you're manufacturing your own products, you can also brand your stock for eBay success. Creating your own brand is a great way to maximize your profits.

979. Choose an easy to remember, catchy name, to stand out from your competition. Think about your niche and try to find a name that suits the topic.

980. Branding can be as easy as placing a sticker on the item to keep things affordable when starting out.

981. As you build your "cluster" of products, your brand will become well known to your regular customers.

982. Having your own brand is far better than a "generic" one if you want to stand above the crowd on eBay. Having your own branded products makes you look professional and more serious about your eBay business.

983. There are no two ways about it... you're always going to have competition when it comes to eBay. What you need to do is constantly watch your competition and make sure you're always one step ahead of them to maximize profits.

984. At least once a week, take a look at what your competition on eBay is doing and how you might come up with something even better to win buyers over.

985. Even if you're lucky enough not to have much competition today, you just never know who's moving into your category and how educated they are in this business. Whatever you do… don't become "complacent" with your eBay business… the minute you take your eye of the ball, you'll go backwards.

986. Competition is healthy and any good seller understands that there are many ways to stand above the crowd. It just takes a little more effort, but it's worth it. Are you prepared to do whatever it takes?

987. Have a look at all the good things your competition does in their business and all the bad things, then see where you can improve what you're doing, so you can blast them out of contention!

988. There are certain strategies that work on eBay and many that don't. As a top seller, it's up to you to keep on top of market changes and eBay changes so that you're always a step ahead of the pack.

989. Giving as much detail about your items as possible and taking clear, close-up pictures from all angles is definitely one way you can move up the ranks.

990. Make sure you're using the right keywords in your title descriptions… this is definitely one area where many sellers get it wrong. Most buyers on eBay search by "product" and not necessarily by "category." This is why using the right keywords is paramount to your selling success.

991. Make sure you have a friendly tone to your copywriting. You'd be blown away at how rude some sellers are and they wonder why they can't dominate their category.

992. Make sure your shipping charges are fair and reasonable. These days buyers are very savvy when it comes to this, so if your competition is way cheaper than you, you're going to struggle.

993. Have you thought about offering bonuses to encourage more shoppers to your eBay business? What bonuses does your competition offer and can you do better?

994. Compare things like photos, copywriting, customer service, warranties, pricing, shipping, etc., to see how you differ from others in your niche.

995. Maybe you could reward your "frequent" shoppers so that they're not lured by new sellers coming into your niche? Everyone likes to feel special and worthwhile, and it doesn't cost much to spoil them.

996. When you send out invoices to your customers, make sure you write a "thank-you note" and a friendly reminder of other things you have that they may be interested in.

997. Check out to see what methods of selling your competition are using. Do they mainly do auctions or buy it now? Do they mix it up and give their customers plenty of options? Make sure you make it as easy as possible to buy from you!

998. Find out if your competition uses the "best offer" option. This is another way to boost sales and profits and I know that many sellers do not offer it. Remember… it's all about maximizing profits in minimum time.

999. Does your competition offer "second chance" offers? Here's a way to make multiple sales from the one finished auction if you're lucky enough to have more of the same item on hand. There's been many an auction where we've sold up to 2 or 3 more items of the same type, simply because we made the second chance offer to bidders who came close to the winning bid.

1000. Make sure you continually test and measure ways of doing things in your eBay business. Keep a close eye on other sellers even in different categories, as you're sure to pick up great ideas!

Within 3 Months Of Starting, We Have A Reliable Revenue Of Over $3,000 Per Month

I wanted to give you feedback on the amazing information that we've received from Matt & Amanda.

My business partner and I attended the eBay Magic course in April 2009, and took a few months to figure out the best niche for us. Once we found it, we were able to apply the tips from your course. It was a topic we were familiar with, so dealing with and meeting customers who also enjoy this product has been a lot of fun.

Within 3 months of starting, we have a reliable revenue of over $3,000 per month, which is profitable. We have managed to dominate the niche and keep testing new ideas to improve.

Each month, we have been able to re-invest profits to expand our offering, and have identified some super-hot items which we are struggling to keep in stock.

We've read and attended other ebay courses, and eBay Magic has by far the most amazing tips and processes to dominate the market. We're excited about growing the business and replicating this success in new niches.

The biggest key tips that you gave, which is where so many other sellers fail, is communication and honesty. These 2 tips alone lead to great feedback and in turn more sales.

Thanks again for your amazing information.

Kind regards

Damian Walker

"Real Success is doing what you love & getting paid for it."

Darren J Stephens
International Bestselling Author & Speaker

Chapter 16

eBay Glossary... What Do All Those Abbreviations Mean?

Chapter 16: eBay Glossary...

1001. **BID**. The amount an eBay member is prepared to place on an auction.

BIN. Buy it now… a fixed price that a buyer can purchase a product for.

BIDDER. An eBay member who bids on an auction therefore entering him / her into a binding contract.

BEST MATCH. The default way in which search results on eBay are organised to help buyers find what they want.

BNWT. Brand new with tags.

NR. No Reserve.

NRFB. Never removed from box.

OB. Original Box.

HTF. Hard to find.

MWMT. Mint with mint tags.

OOAK. One of a kind

PP. PayPal.

SZ. Size.

OOP. Out of print.

TOS. Terms of sale.

NIB. New in box.

MWBT. Mint with both tags.

SCR. Scratch.

NBW. Never been worn.

LTD. Limited.

SFH. Smoke free home.

"Make a decision to be wealthy right now! Most people never decide and that's why they're poor."

Darren J Stephens
International Bestselling Author & Speaker

Chapter 17

Resources & Handy Web Addresses

Chapter 17: Resources & Handy Web Addresses

Compared to running many other business, including traditional and online, eBay has some of the lowest overheads. Not only are their services affordable to get started, compared to other types of business, they have a fantastic array of easy to use and very helpful programs.

It's important that you utilise these helpful resources to help you run your eBay business so you're seen as a professional seller right from day one.

And remember, it's not what it costs you... it's what it can make you! So take advantage of these resources today!

Below you'll find a number of resources we have mentioned throughout the book. Some of the links are quite long, so we've converted them using the tiny URL tool. These links are safe and convenient to use.

Please make the most of the work already done for you to find what you're looking for, simply and easily…

Open an eBay account in your country:

Australia	www.ebay.com.au
USA	www.ebay.com
UK	www.ebay.co.uk

Transfer funds and collect the money:

PayPal	www.paypal.com
PayPal AU	www.paypal.com.au
PayPal UK	www.paypal.co.uk
Transferring Funds	www.travelex.com
Currency Converter	www.xe.com
Skype	www.skype.com

Find any number of web pages within eBay:

eBay Categories	http://hub.shop.ebay.com.au
eBay Glossary	http://tinyurl.com/eBayGlossary
Trading Assistant	http://tinyurl.com/eBayTradingAssistantAU
eBay Selling Fees	http://help.ebay.com.au/Help/Selling/Fees
Site Map	http://pages.ebay.com.au/sitemap.html
Want It Now	http://pages.ebay.com.au/wantitnow
eBay Pulse	http://tinyurl.com/eBayPulseResearch
Deal Finder	http://dealfinder.ebay.com.au/dlf/home
Sell Your Services	http://services.shop.ebay.com.au/
eBay Stores	http://tinyurl.com/eBayStoreSubscriptions
Selling Manager Pro	http://tinyurl.com/SellingManagerPro
PowerSeller Program	http://tinyurl.com/PowerSellerProgram
eBay Toolbar	http://pages.ebay.com.au/ebay_toolbar

Pay Per Click	http://tinyurl.com/ PayPerClickAdCommerce
eBay Guides & Reviews	http://reviews.ebay.com.au
Charity Fundraising	http://pages.ebay.com.au/charity

Use resource tools for listing and research:

Terapeak Research	http://tinyurl.com/BiddingBuzzTerapeak
Auctiva Listing	www.auctiva.com
Escrow Services	https://escrow.com/index.asp
Australia Post	www.auspost.com.au
Going Going Gone	http://tinyurl.com/ GoingGoingGoneArbitraging
World Wide Brands	http://tinyurl.com/OneSourceSuppliers
American Trade Fairs	http://tinyurl.com/AmericanTradeFairs
China Trade Fairs	http://www.cantonfair.org.cn/en/index.asp
Importing Freight Forwarder	www.energylogistics.com.au
Language Translator	www.babblefish.com

Arbitrage websites and product sourcing tools:

Fat Fingers	www.fatfingers.com
Sniping Tool	www.hammersnipe.com
Oztion	www.oztion.com.au
Gumtree	www.gumtree.com.au
Craigslist	www.craigslist.com.au
Liquidation Sourcing	www.liquidation.com

Government and business registration websites:

Register Your Business	www.business.gov.au
Australia Customs	www.customs.gov.au
Apply For ABN	http://tinyurl.com/ApplyForABN
Apply For US Tax ID	http://tinyurl.com/ApplyForTaxID

Database collection and email marketing tool:

Database Program	www.autobusinessmanager.com

And of course the most important tool you could ever invest in, for daily support and guidance to help you achieve your dreams and goals faster and make everything we've discussed in this book a reality:

www.biddingbuzz.com.au

Final Thoughts and Words of Encouragement.

We hope you've really enjoyed reading this book and have taken some great tips on board to help you grow your own exciting, profitable and automated eBay business.

Starting and growing a business of any sort including eBay, takes self-belief, time, dedication, effort and constant action.

By reading this book, you have taken important steps towards creating your own massive success and now all you need to do is stay focused and clear on your outcome.

Keep Learning and growing

Because we've only scratched the surface of what's possible with having an eBay business, it is paramount that you keep learning and following in the steps of others who have the results you're looking for.

Share your dreams with those who encourage you and have your best interests at heart and if possible avoid the ones that tell you that making a great living on eBay is not possible. Anything is possible if you put your mind and heart into it.

If you would like to find out more about our eBay Magic courses and how we mentor people all over the world, go to the link at the bottom of this page and request your free report and DVD valued at $97. We have a team of mentors and course advisors who can point you in the right direction for you if you want to fast track your success.

Get the Best Mentors

The biggest reasons we have been able to fast track our eBay and business success so quickly is because we surround ourselves with the best mentors we can find. No matter where they are in the world!

Have you heard the saying"Success leaves a trail?"We live by this mantra…and if we could offer you one golden gem of advice this would be to follow in the footsteps of only those who have the results you want as no one else is qualified to give you advice. It will save you years of frustration and costly mistakes and make your journey easier.

Remember…you can always get more money but never more time…

Final Thoughts and Words of Encouragement.

Make It Happen For You Now

Tony Robbins says…"You have two things in life…either a result or a story of why things didn't work out for you"…

Right now is your chance to finally get the life you want by taking action and believing it's possible for you.

Of the hundreds of people we mentor, there is one common question that comes up in nearly every conversation when we're helping people become successful.

The question is…"Is it easy, Does it work and Can I do it?"

The answer to that is simply…"If you believe it is possible, follow proven systems and steps, believe in yourself and take the right action…anything is possible."

It's up to you…

See you on top of our eBay Magic Mountain

Warmly,

Matt & Amanda

"Helping You Become Cash & Time Rich with eBay"

FREE BONUS

To Claim Your FREE Report, Your DVD & Special Audio MP3 Gift With A Total Value of **$297** visit...

www.biddingbuzz.com/book

About the Authors

MATT CLARKSON

When Matt Clarkson left school at 16 to become a hands on carpenter the last place you would expect him to end up is running a multinational business specialising in eBay education, but that's exactly what happened.

After initially spending 15 years working in the construction industry on projects ranging from simple homes, mega mansions, high rise commercial buildings and block buster film sets; Matt is now a bestselling author and international expert in Internet Marketing and in particular eBay business development.

His previous experience in construction and Project Management of multimillion dollar mining and construction projects, has enabled him to manage and grow Bidding Buzz from a home based business into a multimillion dollar company in only 3 fast paced years.

After realizing that he needed to make changes in his life and wanting to forge into a brand new industry, Matt and his partner Amanda began selling on eBay in early 2006 and quickly established themselves as one of Australia's fastest growing eBay businesses.

They had actually created one of the world's leading eBay business systems, enabling people to establish and automate their eBay business up to 90%. It was only a matter of time before they knew they had to share this system with the world and quickly built Bidding Buzz into a global corporation, with successful and happy customers all over the world.

Now with students in Australia, the United States, the United Kingdom, Ireland, Hong Kong, Indonesia, Sweden, Malaysia and beyond, with a support team of 16 staff members, Matt along with Amanda, is leading the Bidding Buzz phenomenon across the globe. The future is looking bright not only for Bidding Buzz, but for the thousands of people who have now studied their eBay business systems and are making positive changes for themselves and their families.

AMANDA CLARKSON

Amanda is a passionate entrepreneur who left school at age 16 and has had 33 jobs and has gone on to establish and run 11 businesses over the last 20 years.

Amanda's eBay business, which she started with a credit card in Feb 06 was a run away success and is still forging ahead to this day. Now, along with her husband Matt, she shows everyday people how to become cash and time rich with eBay through their simple, and inspiring eBay education courses.

This amazing journey has seen her now present to thousands of people, from all walks of life, ages and backgrounds around the world, including Australia, London and America.

As a result, everyday people are now living the 'eBay lifestyle' enjoying more time and more income for themselves and their families.

Her deep desire to help and inspire people to improve their lives both financially and personally, coupled with the powerful Bidding Buzz eBay education programs, has driven her to the top of the business and online community around the world.

Amanda's vision is to help as many people as possible live life more on their own terms instead of someone else's through The Magic Of Making Money On eBay.